# MEET THE AUTHORS

25 Writers of Upper Elementary and
Middle School Books Talk About Their Work

# MEET THE AUTHORS

25 Writers of Upper Elementary and
Middle School Books Talk About Their Work

*by Deborah Kovacs*

SCHOLASTIC
PROFESSIONAL BOOKS

NEW YORK • TORONTO • LONDON • AUCKLAND • SYDNEY

*For Niko who has always been there*

Cover design by Frank Maiocco and Vincent Ceci
Cover illustration by Chi Chung
Interior design by Solutions by Design, Inc.
Photo research by Daniella Jo Nilva

ISBN 0-590-49476-7

12 11 10 9 8 7 6 5 4 3 2          6/9

Printed in the U.S.A.

# Contents

Preface . . . . . . . . . . . . . . . . . . . . . . . . . . . . . . . . . . . . . . . . . . . . . . . . . . . . . . . . . . 7

**THE AUTHORS**

Avi . . . . . . . . . . . . . . . . . . . . . . . . . . . . . . . . . . . . . . . . . . . . . . . . . . . . . . . . . . . 8

James Lincoln Collier and Christopher Collier . . . . . . . . . . . . . . . . . . . . . . 12

Susan Cooper . . . . . . . . . . . . . . . . . . . . . . . . . . . . . . . . . . . . . . . . . . . . . . 16

Robert Cormier . . . . . . . . . . . . . . . . . . . . . . . . . . . . . . . . . . . . . . . . . . . . 20

Chris Crutcher . . . . . . . . . . . . . . . . . . . . . . . . . . . . . . . . . . . . . . . . . . . . 24

Paul Fleischman . . . . . . . . . . . . . . . . . . . . . . . . . . . . . . . . . . . . . . . . . . . 28

Paula Fox . . . . . . . . . . . . . . . . . . . . . . . . . . . . . . . . . . . . . . . . . . . . . . . . 32

S. E. Hinton . . . . . . . . . . . . . . . . . . . . . . . . . . . . . . . . . . . . . . . . . . . . . . 36

Will Hobbs . . . . . . . . . . . . . . . . . . . . . . . . . . . . . . . . . . . . . . . . . . . . . . . 40

M. E. Kerr (Marijane Meaker) . . . . . . . . . . . . . . . . . . . . . . . . . . . . . . . . . 44

Julius Lester . . . . . . . . . . . . . . . . . . . . . . . . . . . . . . . . . . . . . . . . . . . . . . 48

Janet Taylor Lisle . . . . . . . . . . . . . . . . . . . . . . . . . . . . . . . . . . . . . . . . . . 52

Margaret Mahy . . . . . . . . . . . . . . . . . . . . . . . . . . . . . . . . . . . . . . . . . . . . 56

Gloria D. Miklowitz . . . . . . . . . . . . . . . . . . . . . . . . . . . . . . . . . . . . . . . . 60

Nicholasa Mohr . . . . . . . . . . . . . . . . . . . . . . . . . . . . . . . . . . . . . . . . . . . 64

Michael Morpurgo . . . . . . . . . . . . . . . . . . . . . . . . . . . . . . . . . . . . . . . . . 68

Katherine Paterson . . . . . . . . . . . . . . . . . . . . . . . . . . . . . . . . . . . . . . . . . 72

Richard Peck . . . . . . . . . . . . . . . . . . . . . . . . . . . . . . . . . . . . . . . . . . . . . 76

Robert Newton Peck . . . . . . . . . . . . . . . . . . . . . . . . . . . . . . . . . . . . . . . . 80

William Sleator . . . . . . . . . . . . . . . . . . . . . . . . . . . . . . . . . . . . . . . . . . . . 84

Todd Strasser . . . . . . . . . . . . . . . . . . . . . . . . . . . . . . . . . . . . . . . . . . . . . 88

Joyce Carol Thomas . . . . . . . . . . . . . . . . . . . . . . . . . . . . . . . . . . . . . . . . 92

Patricia Wrightson . . . . . . . . . . . . . . . . . . . . . . . . . . . . . . . . . . . . . . . . . 96

Jane Yolen . . . . . . . . . . . . . . . . . . . . . . . . . . . . . . . . . . . . . . . . . . . . . . . 100

Paul Zindel . . . . . . . . . . . . . . . . . . . . . . . . . . . . . . . . . . . . . . . . . . . . . . 104

# Preface

The authors you are about to meet write for many reasons, but each would probably agree with this statement: they write to make a difference. None of them realistically hopes their writing will solve our world's problems. But all know how hard it is to grow up. No question I asked elicited more deep sighs and heartfelt responses than: "What do you think can be done to help young people today?"

Each of these writers has chosen the gifts of a writer's sensibility and story-shaping talent to try to make the world a more understandable place for young people. For this, and for their many, varied, imaginative approaches to this important task, this talented group have earned my deepest respect.

Some authors profiled, such as Robert Cormier and S. E. Hinton, may already be familiar to you. Others, like Patricia Wrightson and Michael Morpurgo, though well-known in their own countries, may be new discoveries. Some authors, such as Paul Zindel and M. E. Kerr, have been writing for a very long time, while others, like Chris Crutcher and Will Hobbs, are relatively new on the scene. Each author selected for this book has been included because in my opinion, and that of the many teachers, librarians, booksellers, editors and students with whom I consulted, they have important things to say, and say them spectacularly well.

This book can be used in two ways: to give a reader background and insight to the writing approaches taken by an author whose book is being read; or to make known new or unfamiliar writers. The writing activities that accompany each profile were designed by the writers themselves. Their voices come through in the activities, I believe, and so offer students a chance to extend their connection with an author they've come to know.

The group of people you're about to meet leave me hopeful about the future and about the power good books have to make strong and lasting impressions. In their work and in their words, I hope you will find new worlds, and maybe even answers to questions that lie deep in your own heart.

Enjoy the journey!

Deborah Kovacs

# Avi

**BORN:** December 27, 1937, in Brooklyn, New York
**CURRENT HOME:** Providence, Rhode Island

## SELECTED TITLES

**Something Upstairs: A Tale of Ghosts**
1988

**The Man Who Was Poe**
1989

**The True Confessions of Charlotte Doyle**
1990

**Windcatcher**
1991

**Nothing but the Truth**
1991

**"Who Was That Masked Man, Anyway?"**
1992

**Blue Heron**
1992

**City of Light/City of Dark**
1993

**Judy and Punch**
1993

**The Bird, the Frog and the Light**
1994

**The Barn**
1994

Avi was born in Brooklyn, New York, just before World War II. He grew up surrounded by an extended family that included his parents and a twin sister, and aunts, uncles, and grandparents who lived nearby. Many members of Avi's family were writers, including two of his great-grandfathers, his grandmother, an aunt, his parents, and his twin sister. Understandably, Avi wanted to be a writer, too. Though a big reader, he was discouraged from writing by his family because of a writing disability called *dysgraphia*. Avi's learning disability causes him to reverse letters and misspell words. "One of my aunts said I could spell a four-letter word wrong five ways," he said.

## OVERCOMING ADVERSITY

At school, teachers thought Avi was sloppy and that he didn't pay attention. His papers would be returned to him covered with the red ink of corrections. It bothered Avi a lot. "I think there was so much criticism, I just stopped listening to it," he says. "*I* liked what *I* wrote." His problems with dysgraphia even led him to flunk out of one school, but Avi continued to believe in himself.

Between two years of high school, a summer tutor finally taught Avi that writing was not an end in itself, but a way to communicate. He was also encouraged by a friend of the family named Lee Hays. "I was always eager for anyone to take me seriously," Avi remembers. "And Lee did, for whatever reasons. To be taken seriously was an enormous thing for me."

> *"I think there was so much criticism, I just stopped listening to it."*

When Avi was around seventeen, Lee would read what Avi had written, then discuss it. Lee said two things to Avi that the author remembers to this day. "I came home from college and gave him five plays I had written," says Avi. "I asked him if he would read them. It seems ridiculous now, but he said, 'Come back in a couple of days.' " Lee didn't read all of the plays, but he read enough to get an impression of how Avi's writing was progressing. Avi came back to hear Lee's opinion, which was: "It takes a heap of manure to make a flower grow! Keep working!"

Another time, Lee gave Avi more important advice. He said: "If you want to be a writer, you have to go to bed thinking what you've done is the greatest writing in the world, as long as when you wake up in the morning, you know it's the worst. If you reverse the two, you're in trouble."

## STARTING WITH PICTURE BOOKS

Avi wasn't able to devote all his time to being a writer. Though writing was always his main interest, he worked as a librarian, too, for twenty-five years. He spent years writing the first 800 pages of his "great American novel," never really finishing it. Then, a friend encouraged Avi to contact children's book publishers, and before long, his first children's book, the picture book *Things That Sometimes Happen* was published. After writing a few more picture books, Avi wrote a novel called *No More Magic.*

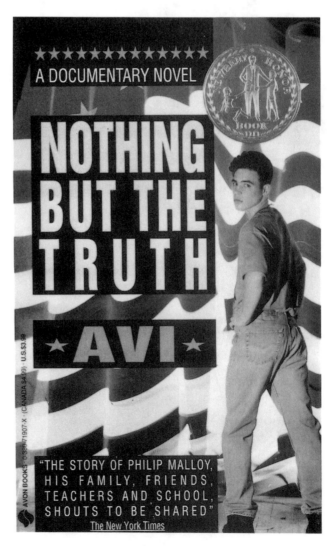

★ ★ ★ ★ ★ ★ ★ ★ ★ ★ ★ ★ ★
A DOCUMENTARY NOVEL

NOTHING BUT THE TRUTH

★AVI★

"THE STORY OF PHILIP MALLOY, HIS FAMILY, FRIENDS, TEACHERS AND SCHOOL, SHOUTS TO BE SHARED"
The New York Times

A spellbinding tale of intrigue and murder on the high seas

*The True Confessions of Charlotte Doyle*

by award-winning author Avi

## SPOTLIGHT ON:
### THE TRUE CONFESSIONS OF CHARLOTTE DOYLE

Travel back in time to the nineteenth century with 13-year-old Charlotte Doyle, the high-spirited heroine of this seafaring adventure. Charlotte's "confessions" are told in the form of a recollection that describe her transatlantic trip from England to America. The sole female aboard a ship full of men, Charlotte is quickly drawn into the middle of a desperate situation. The satisfying ending develops from the heroine's quick thinking and plucky nerve. A suspense-filled nautical tale for every young reader.

He was very satisfied with the process of writing a novel. "Plus, it turned out to be a decent book and was well received. "Success makes you feel comfortable with what you're doing," he says. For more than twenty years, he has written books, mostly novels, in addition to some short stories and even a comic book. (Avi loved reading comic books when he was a kid.)

## LETTING A STORY FIND ITSELF

Avi says that he "writes slowly, quickly." He finds writing a long, laborious process. "Usually I start at page one and work to the end of the book. But that's very misleading, because I'll get to page forty and go back and rewrite page two to accommodate page forty, so it's always back and forth, back and forth. I rewrite the books forty or fifty times. I really do."

He often waits to describe his characters' appearance until he has rewritten the book a number of times. "I don't know what they look like," he says. "They change when I go back over the book and look at what I've written."

> *"I rewrite the books forty or fifty times. I really do."*

The setting of the story is very important to Avi. "I don't imagine places," he says. "I have to have a very concrete sense of place. I tend to write about where I'm living." He often buys maps of places or even draws maps, if necessary.

The final story is often very different from the first draft. "The first draft is so crude, it's awful," says Avi. Changes come as he reacts to what he has written. "I believe that writing is actually very easy. The hard part is reading your own work critically." Avi thinks writers can get clues for rewriting by carefully reading their works in progress and trying to find ways to help the reader see, feel, and experience the situations. In revision, he works hard to do this. He also tries to pull things out of his stories, to make his stories richer.

> *"I have to have a very concrete sense of place. I tend to write about where I'm living."*

An example of this is in *The True Confessions of Charlotte Doyle*. It's the story of a thirteen-year-old girl who is the sole passenger and only female on a transatlantic voyage from England to America in 1832. A mutiny erupts during the voyage. From an upper-class family herself, Charlotte sides at first with the aristocratic captain. But she comes to realize that he is cruel and unfair. She eventually sides with the ship's crew and becomes attached to them.

## WORDS FROM THE AUTHOR:

*"People don't know what to expect when they pick up one of my books. I'm always changing styles. Sometimes people are put off by this constant changing. Other people applaud it."*

Says Avi, "My favorite part of the book is when Charlotte says good-bye to the crew the night before she gets off the ship. I worked on that book for three years. That part wasn't in it until the last month."

Avi's editor read the manuscript, which was originally written without that scene, and noticed that a farewell was missing. "The minute he said that to me, I knew he was right," says Avi. "It took a couple of minutes to write, but the point was I knew these characters so well that I could literally insert the scene into the book. It was written separately from the rest of the story." Avi says this part of the book is his favorite, not necessarily because it was the best, but because "I was saying good-bye to her, too." ∎

## A WRITING ACTIVITY
### from Avi

In three sentences or less, describe the room in which you sleep. Make your description so vivid that somebody who has never seen your room will know what it looks like.

# James Lincoln Collier
# Christopher Collier

**BORN:** (James) June 27, 1928; (Christopher) January 29, 1930, both in New York, New York

**CURRENT HOMES:** (James) Pawling, New York; (Christopher) Orange, Connecticut

## SELECTED TITLES

**Jump Ship to Freedom**
1981

**War Comes to Willy Freeman**
1983

**My Brother Sam Is Dead**
1984

**Who Is Carrie?**
1984

**The Bloody Country**
1985

**The Winter Hero**
1985

**The Clock**
1992

**With Every Drop of Blood**
1994

*(Note: Each of the Colliers has written books on their own. These are the books they have coauthored.)*

To write about the past, believes historian Christopher Collier, you must put your mind back into the time and place you're focusing on. "There are two tasks," he says of writing historical fiction. "The first is to bring the perspective of the present to bear on the past. The second is to get inside the minds of those people."

Christopher and his brother, James Lincoln Collier, have created many believable characters and placed them in significant events in American history. The authors have written about an escaped slave (*Jump Ship to Freedom*), a boy during the revolutionary war (*My Brother Sam Is Dead*), a boy in Shay's Rebellion

James Lincoln Collier

Christopher Collier

(*The Winter Hero*), among many others.

## DIVIDING THE WORK

How do the two writers collaborate on one book? Each has a specific task. The idea for the book usually comes from Christopher. Christopher suggests a topic, then James responds to the idea. If he's interested in it, "we talk about it and decide if we'll go ahead," says James. For example, Christopher once suggested they write a story based on a true incident in which a slave sued his master and won. That book developed into *Jump Ship to Freedom*.

Next, Christopher dives into research, about which he is meticulous. He combs archives to find primary sources, such as letters, diaries, and eyewitness accounts. In the end, the books are as thoroughly researched as the scholarly books and articles Christopher writes as an historian. "If we say in the story it snowed three inches on January 4, 1787, in Springfield, Massachusetts, then you can be sure it really did," says Christopher.

Sometimes Christopher has to learn about things that traditional historians might not necessarily explore. "For one book I needed to know how to spin wool," says Christopher. "Do you sit or stand? How do you move?" For that research he traveled to Old Sturbridge Village in Massachusetts, a living museum of life in the 1830s, where he read books, talked to the curators, and guides, and inspected the spinning wheels himself.

Viewing actual objects and documents from a time period gives the writer a window on the past. "Sometimes I'll read something in a diary or handle

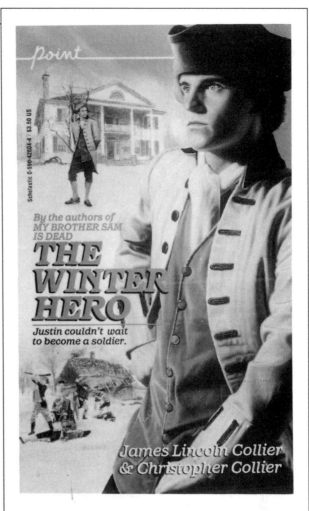

By the authors of MY BROTHER SAM IS DEAD

## THE WINTER HERO

*Justin couldn't wait to become a soldier.*

James Lincoln Collier & Christopher Collier

## SPOTLIGHT ON:
### THE WINTER HERO

After the American Revolution was over, things were still far from settled in our country. This book tells the story of Justin, a boy who took part in Shay's Rebellion, an uprising of farmers who were afraid of losing their property rights. As he helps the farmers in the Rebellion, Justin has a chance to save the life of his sister's husband, Peter, whom he idolizes.

something from the past and I get a flash of insight," Christopher says. "One of the things I learned at Sturbridge was how tedious it must have been to spin wool all day long. That helps me understand that for a person of that time, a new shirt was an amazing thing. Think of the hours that went into making it: shearing the wool, carding it, spinning it into yarn, weaving it, sewing it."

When the research is complete, Christopher works out the structure of the book. "I prepare a story outline based on these historical materials, including the characters. I provide all of the research material I think would be necessary to write the book." He also collects visual material such as maps and drawings of the clothes of that time.

Christopher brings his outline and all of the reference material to James'

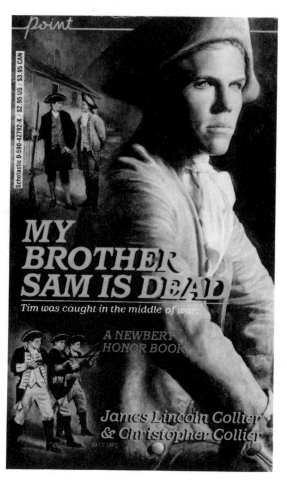

home, an hour away. The brothers review the material and the proposed structure, and James reviews what he thinks will and won't work. "The story has to be congruent with the historical basis," says James. "But it has to be exciting and dramatic, too."

Christopher's task is over. Now it's James' turn. "I sit down and write the book just as if I had written the outline myself," says James. "But I take lots of liberties with what he has given me. If I feel something is going to work better than what he's suggested, I put that in. I don't feel constrained."

After James writes the first draft, the brothers get together again and go over the manuscript. Occasionally, Christopher changes some of the dialogue. But virtually all of the words in the book are written by James.

## LIVING THE EVENTS

Though he has been a writer all his life, it is still hard work for James. To get the process going, he has to focus on the project. "I exclude everything," he says. "I get myself into the story so that I'm living the events, so that I can see everything, smell everything, hear the people talking. Once I get into that state, I write as fast as I can." Writing this way

### WORDS FROM JAMES LINCOLN COLLIER:

"Our father was a cowboy. He wrote western fiction until the Depression came along. Then he couldn't earn a living at it any more. He became a tree surgeon."

can be a tense experience. "It's like playing jazz," says James, who plays the jazz trombone. "If you get out there and coast, it's not going to be very powerful. You may have a good time, but you need a certain amount of intensity to make it sound effective." Those intense days, when he's writing for five or six hours every day, are "not very much fun," says James.

## FAMILY OF WRITERS

The Colliers descend from a long line of writers. Of this James once said, "I thus became a writer the way other young people go into the family business. It never occurred to me that I couldn't write; it was what people did, and it has been what I have done since I became an adult."

> "I get myself into the story so that I'm living the events, so that I can see everything, smell everything, hear the people talking. Once I get into that state, I write as fast as I can."

As a child, Christopher was late learning to read. "But once I learned, I read a lot," he says. Christopher went on to become editor of his high school and college newspapers.

When they were growing up, the Colliers spent time in the home of their uncle, William Slater Brown, who in the 1920s and 1930s was part of a group of writers known as the "Lost Generation."

## A WRITING ACTIVITY
### from James Lincoln Collier

Think of a strong emotion you once felt, such as anger, jealousy, love, or hate. Write down how that emotion affected you physically. Did your face turn red? Did your heart beat fast? Did your limbs feel weak? Did you pace the floor? Imagine that a character feels the same way. Write a scene in which the character displays this feeling. What does the character say? How does the character behave? Show your readers.

The group included John Dos Passos, Malcolm Cowley, and Hart Crane. James now owns his uncle's house, spending weekends there. James enjoys thinking of the house's literary history. "Hart Crane wrote portions of *The Bridge* in my bedroom!" he says. "For a period of time in the twenties and thirties, this house was a hangout for some very interesting people."

Best friends all their lives, the Collier brothers clearly work well together. The process is basically smooth. Inevitably, though, disagreements sometimes crop up. How are they resolved? "He's older and bigger than me and he can beat me up," says Christopher of his brother, laughing. "When we were kids, he always won every argument. He might not agree with that, but that's how it seemed to me." ■

# Susan Cooper

**BORN:** May 23, 1935, in Burnham, Buckinghamshire, England
**CURRENT HOME:** Cambridge, Massachusetts

## SELECTED TITLES

### FOR YOUNG ADULT

**Over Sea, Under Stone**
1966

**The Dark Is Rising**
1973

**The Grey King**
1975

**Dawn of Fear**
1980

**Seaward**
1983

**Greenwitch**
1985

**Silver on a Tree**
1987

### FOR CHILDREN

**The Silver Cow**
1983

**The Selkie Girl**
1986

**Tam Lin**
1991

**Danny and the Kings**
1993

**Matthew's Dragon**
1994

As a twelve-year-old girl in England, Susan Cooper went with her grandfather to see a film called *A Matter of Life and Death*. (In the United States, it was called *Stairway to Heaven*.) "The film has had more influence on my writing than anything else I have ever read, seen, or heard," she says.

The story is about an English World War II fighter pilot who is about to crash. As the film begins, he is talking on his radio to an American girl who is stationed in London.

Susan says, "The fantasy of the film is that he is supposed to die, and he doesn't. He finds himself on a beach. He thinks he's in heaven, but in fact, he's in Devon. It turns out that the conductor, who was supposed to take him to another world, did not. He wasn't thinking hard enough."

Why was this film, which Susan calls a "many-layered fantasy," so important to her? "It must have shown me what you can do by interweaving the real and the fantastic," she says. To this day, she doesn't really understand why the film affected her as it did. But she says, "You should expose yourself to as many possible influences as you can while you're growing up. By accident, something may have an effect."

The fantasies Susan has written have had powerful effects on many of her readers. "I once got a letter from a girl in her mid-teens who was passionate about my Dark Is Rising series (which includes *Over Sea, Under Stone*; *The Dark Is Rising*; *Greenwitch*; *The Grey King*; and *Silver on a Tree*)." The girl wrote, "Those books changed my life."

To the author of those books, this was unnerving. Susan contemplates, amazed, the way "some accident will present a particular work of art, painting, book, or piece of music to a developing mind or imagination at just the right moment, and the imagination will seize it and make it its own."

## A WARTIME CHILDHOOD

Susan grew up in Buckinghamshire, just outside of London, during World War II. She remembers the sounds of air-raid sirens and of bombs falling. She especially remembers a night when she was six years old, returning to her home from an air-raid shelter. Her father pulled back the blackout curtains to reveal, on the distant skyline, the city of London in flames. "During that period of the Blitz," she has written, "in the first three months alone, more than 36,000 bombs were dropped on the London area, and 12,696 civilians were killed and 20,000 seriously injured. My parents were Londoners; they wanted me to remember."

The image lasted in her mind, and she put elements of it into *Dawn of Fear*, and, she suspects, into many other books she wrote. The wartime years also gave her imagination, and in her writing, a strongly defined sense of Us against Them, Good against Evil, and the

Forces of Light against the Forces of Darkness.

Susan doesn't know at what moment she realized she was a writer. She says, "the only possible answer is—it just happened." As a young child, she wrote plays as well as a weekly newspaper, and even a book.

## UNIVERSITY DAYS

At Oxford University, Susan attended lectures given by C. S. Lewis, author of the Chronicles of Narnia series, and J. R. R. Tolkein, who was just completing his Lord of the Rings books. Though her writing has been compared to that of both fantasy writers, she was not aware of any particular influence they had upon her at the time. She remembers them as "chunky, pipe-smoking dons." She didn't even realize until much later that C. S. Lewis wrote novels for children.

Susan worked as a journalist for a number of years after college. One of her bosses in those days was the writer Ian Fleming, who became famous for his books about 007—the secret agent James Bond. Susan wrote her first novels in those years, too. With her career as a writer and journalist in London in full bloom, she surprised many people when, at the age of twenty-seven, she married a man almost twenty years older than herself and moved to the United States.

## A WRITER'S IMAGINATION

For the first few years in

## SPOTLIGHT ON:
### *OVER SEA, UNDER STONE*

The first title in Susan's five-volume, award-winning Dark Is Rising series, this book tells the story of two brothers and a sister—Simon, Barnabas, and Jane Drew. They find a clue to an ancient hidden treasure in the attic of their home. The treasure has magical powers against an evil force called the Dark, which has warred with its enemy, the Light, throughout history. The Drews find the treasure and defeat the forces of the Dark.

these influences were working together. A great series of books was brewing.

On a "very peculiar" day she'll never forget, a vision of the entire five-volume Dark Is Rising series came to her, almost at once. It began with the image of a boy who wakes up on his birthday and discovers he can work magic. Of this, she has written, "It was, I saw now, just a part of something larger, something that seemed to have been waiting for me to be ready to look at it." Susan remembers sitting there thinking about this image and gradually realizing that she was seeing the image not just of one book, but of a whole series of books, beginning with *Over Sea, Under Stone*, which she had published seven years earlier as—she thought then—an independent novel.

"I took a piece of paper and scribbled down four titles, four outlines, with characters, plots, and settings—very rough, very brief, but definite." Then she wrote the last page of the last book in the series. In that brief session, she had defined what would become a major portion of the writing for which she will be remembered always.

Susan says that ideas for her books are "very dream-based." Not that she's actually sleeping when she conceives of a story. Rather, she feels as though she watches her stories grow, "It's very much like a dream, except I'm guiding it." When she gets ready to write, she feels herself in a state of agitation. "I feel as though my imagination were pregnant— there's a baby in there, kicking."

She says that for her, writing a book is like a journey, with many surprises along the way. "I know where I'm starting from. I know where I'm going. I

America, Susan was busy raising a family and continuing to write. She also read a lot about English history and folktales. Susan was homesick for her native country and went back often to visit. Somehow, deep in her imagination, all of know roughly who's going with me. But I don't know who I'm going to meet."

Susan writes in notebooks. "The text is on the right-hand side," she says. "On the left are little notes to myself. I can be writing one chapter, and suddenly an image or an idea emerges for something a couple of chapters ahead." She is interrupted by the idea. She writes it down on the left-hand side, "to keep it safe," and goes on with her story.

*"[When I'm writing a book] I know where I'm starting from. I know where I'm going. I know roughly who's going with me. But I don't know who I'm going to meet."*

Susan believes that writing is hard work. "Most of writing is just slogging away," she says. But there are good days. "If you pay your dues to the muse long enough, she will reward you." On those good days, Susan says, quoting her friend, actor Hume Cronyn, "the writing just comes out of my arm."

Susan reads a lot, "to hear the echoes of writing." She believes that "all people draw upon a basic accumulation of stories, images, and patterns of story we have probably been developing as long as we've been able to think." She calls this notion, quoting J. R. R. Tolkein, "the cauldron of story," and says that she reads to try to find "the right ingredients for the particular soup that's in the ladle."

What advice does Susan offer would-be writers? "I would discourage them

from becoming writers. It's such a difficult way of life. If they are discouraged, and they are true writers, they will write anyway, and they will have proved they had the stamina you need in order to survive as a writer, by breaking through the discouragement." She also hopes that those who want to write will "read, read, read. Everything. It is essential to be soaked in reading if you want to write."

Susan adds: "It is that vast amount of words in stories, especially the sound of words, that turned me into a writer. If I have any virtues as a writer, they come from all the reading I have done. You can't write words that sound the way they ought to unless you have been soaked in a lot of other words that sound beautiful." ∎

## A WRITING ACTIVITY
### from Susan Cooper

Think of a character who is going on a perfectly ordinary trip somewhere. Imagine something quite extraordinary that happens to him or her on the way. Make it take the story into a totally different world.

# Robert Cormier

**BORN:** January 17, 1925, in Leominster, Massachusetts
**CURRENT HOME:** Leominster, Massachusetts

Halfway through *I Am the Cheese*, Bob Cormier realized he wanted to place an actual phone number in the story as part of the plot. He knew that his readers might actually dial that number one day, so he had to be careful which one he chose. "I could have used that fake 555 number that many writers use," he says, referring to a nonexistent exchange. "Or I could have made up an entirely different phone number. But what if that really belonged to someone who wouldn't welcome many calls?" The solution? "I put in my own phone number." No sooner was the book published, when his phone started ringing off the hook. And it hasn't stopped since. The author estimates that thousands of kids have called him over the years.

Being this available to his readers (in spite of the occasional inconvenience) is rewarding to Bob. "As a writer, I can't afford to be a recluse or not involved with life," he says.

Because his readers must sense that he's on their side, they aren't afraid to contact him. Sometimes one of his readers phones for an important reason. "A girl in Connecticut—I knew she had emotional problems—called me," he remembers. "She identified with Adam in *I Am the Cheese*." (In that novel, the main character has lost track of his own identity.) Bob talked with the girl for half an hour. Later, he got in touch with a former teacher of hers, letting

## SELECTED TITLES

**The Chocolate War**
1974

**I Am the Cheese**
1977

**After the First Death**
1979

**Eight Plus One**
1980

**Beyond the Chocolate War**
1986

**Fade**
1989

**The Bumblebee Flies Anyway**
1991

**Now and at the Hour**
1991

**We All Fall Down**
1993

**I Have Words to Spend**
1994

the teacher know the girl needed help.

## EARLY YEARS

Bob grew up during the Great Depression, in a poor French Canadian neighborhood called French Hill in the city of Leominster, Massachusetts, a town that he renamed Monument in his books. He was a great reader as a child and fondly remembers his youth in a large, loving family. Of his childhood, he says, "I was a skinny kid, shy and introverted, who worked to put all my longings and yearnings on paper."

The library was his home away from home. He read through the entire children's section quickly, then moved on to books by such writers as Thomas Wolfe and Ernest Hemingway. Thomas Wolfe, Bob says, "opened the door emotionally for me as a writer" and Ernest Hemingway "opened it stylistically. Hemingway made me realize you don't have to have a mountain of prose. You can write in a clear, thin stream. Hemingway used simple words in his writing. He made me realize that the one great adjective, or the one great verb can do the job. You don't need all these other words."

While still very young, Bob realized another critical aspect of writing: the

## SPOTLIGHT ON: *THE BUMBLEBEE FLIES ANYWAY*

Which of Bob Cormier's books does he wish more of his readers knew about? "My neglected child is *The Bumblebee Flies Anyway.* I really love that book. I love all my books. But this book has been neglected. I think it's a very effective novel. It has a lot of values in it. It deals with identity. I recommend it."

importance of metaphor and simile. "I discovered those techniques as a teenager," he says. He was writing a story based on a situation in his own life. It was about a boy with a crush on a girl from the other side of town. Like that character, Bob lived on the poor side of town and liked a girl from a wealthy family. "I wanted to describe the big, beautiful house she lived in. I found it was impossible, because I knew nothing about architecture. I didn't know what kind of a house it was." He remembers walking along the streets of his neighborhood in despair, thinking "I want to be a writer, and I can't even describe a house." Then he had a brainstorm! "This is about a thirteen-year-old kid. He's the narrator. He's writing in the first person. He doesn't know about houses, either!" Bob hurried home and wrote "She lived in a great big white birthday cake of a house." It worked.

At that moment, Bob discovered the power of figures of speech, similes, and metaphors. He relies on those techniques to this day. "Instead of describing a building, I'll use a metaphor," he says. "I want to get on with the story. I let character come out of action, rather than description, and let characters be judged by what they do, not by what they look like, what they say, or where they come from."

## A PROFESSIONAL WORDSMITH

After college, Bob decided he wanted to support himself by working with words. He began as a reporter for a radio station in Worcester, Massachusetts. Later he became a newspaper reporter and editor at the *Worcester Telegram*, remaining in the newspaper business for thirty years. Was he a "hard-boiled journalist" in those days? "I *banged* around a lot," he says with a laugh. "I covered all the beats. I started with police and fire, then went into political reporting."

Bob loved being a street reporter. "I worked the night beat on the *Telegram* for seven years," he says. "That's when all the stuff really happens." Working nights, Bob wrote fiction during the day. "A lot of people said to me, 'How can you write all day at work and then come home and write some more?'

But the writing at work was factual, and the other was creative. It was like dessert." After *I Am the Cheese* was published in 1977, Bob quit journalism to devote himself full-time to creating fiction.

In his fiction, characters are always more important to him than the stories' plots or settings. "You've got to create characters that readers either love or hate, or else the greatest writing and the greatest plot in the world won't work." Bob says he's always been interested in "the human interest part of things, the human factor."

## WHATEVER HAPPENED TO ARCHIE?

Often, Bob's characters surprise even him. "The thing you try to avoid in writing is a cliche'd character," he says. Some of his characters fascinate him so much, he keeps writing about them, years after the books are published. "Even though I don't plan to publish any of that stuff," he says, "every once in a while, when whatever I'm working on has run out of twists and turns, I'll write about a character I really love."

One such character is Archie, the villain of *The Chocolate War*, whose cruel manipulations terrorize an entire school. "I've written about him when he was eight-years-old. I've written about him when he was twenty-eight," says Bob. For those who wonder what became of Archie after high school, Bob

**WORDS FROM THE AUTHOR:**
"Writing a story is like going down a path in the woods. You follow the path. You don't worry about getting lost, you just go."

offers a few clues. "He would be, from what I've written, on the fringes of politics. He's not a politician himself. He's behind the scenes, pulling strings. Always, always the string puller."

*"As a writer, I can't afford to be a recluse, or not involved with life."*

Were Archie's best years the ones in high school? Certainly, says Bob. "There's a sadness about him after high school. He's like the guy who did the fifty-yard run in football as a senior and still sits around talking about it when he's forty-nine. That's Archie. Still clever, but things were never in his control again the way they were at Trinity."

Where did the Archie character come from? "My son Peter was going to a high school much like the school in the book. As a fund-raising event, they were having a chocolate sale, and Peter refused to sell the chocolates. He was the only kid in the place who didn't sell the chocolates. Nothing happened to him but something happened to me. I used a technique many writers use: 'What if? What if there had been peer pressure on the boy? What if there had been faculty pressure?'" The story grew from there.

## A WRITER'S TASKS

When he writes, Bob attempts two things: "I'm trying to grab the reader, keep ahead of the reader, and provide the unexpected. That leads to the stuff that even surprises me," he says.

Bob approaches his writing in a very businesslike manner. "I usually get to the typewriter by 8:30 A.M., whether I feel like it or not," he says. "Some times I do, some times I don't." On occasion, the distance from the easy chair to the typewriter is the longest trek in the world, he finds. As he walks, he transforms himself into a writer. "The magic happens to me when I'm at the typewriter," he says. "That's when these characters take off and the twists appear."

In his first drafts, Bob lets his writing flow, trying to capture the scenes swirling around his imagination. Then he rewrites—mostly to pare his story but sometimes to get a passage just right. "I do a lot of rewriting, because sometimes the first draft doesn't gel. It doesn't sound right. I do it over until I get that satisfying click that tells me 'this works.'" ■

## A WRITING ACTIVITY
### from Bob Cormier

Find a passage in a book you love in which there's an emotional scene for your favorite character. Notice that the writer *conveys* the emotion through the action and dialogue, but doesn't *tell* you what emotion you should feel.

Think of a new situation for that character. Does he lose his girlfriend? Get into a fight? Write a new scene. Try to capture the emotion without using words like *scared*, *sad*, or *happy*.

# Chris Crutcher

**BORN:** July 17, 1946, in Cascade, Idaho
**CURRENT HOME:** Spokane, Washington

**W**hat is Chris Crutcher's favorite comment by a reader? "A girl in Houston came up to me after a talk. Everybody else had gone away," reports Chris. "She said, 'I don't have a question. I just want you to know I read *Chinese Handcuffs* and I thought you knew me.'"

*Chinese Handcuffs* deals with a number of painful subjects, including molestation. The girl at the meeting had been molested, Chris learned, but had been initially afraid to share her secret. "One of the things that happened when she read the book was it gave her a way to talk about the experience," says Chris. "Luckily, her teacher was somebody she felt she could talk with." Chris was glad his writing was able to help someone in trouble.

As a counselor to teens for over twenty years, Chris says he knows a lot about kids. He knows how they turn out if they haven't been loved as young children and especially if they've been abused. "There's a look of emptiness or toughness that covers fear and a struggle for some kind of voice, a struggle for wanting your life, your existence, to have impact," he says.

One reason Chris first started writing was to help kids in trouble. He wanted to reach those who were hurting, he says, to provide a magnet for youngsters who had difficulty dealing with their feelings. "Hard times are magnetic to hard times," he says, suggesting that kids who are suffering may gravitate to his stories and be helped.

## SELECTED TITLES

**Running Loose**
1983

**Stotan!**
1986

**The Crazy Horse Electric Game**
1987

**Chinese Handcuffs**
1989

**Athletic Shorts: Six Short Stories**
1991

**The Deep End: A Novel of Suspense**
1992

**Iron Man**
1995

## AEROBICS FOR THE HEAD

When he's getting ready to write a book, Chris begins by mulling over the story in his mind while he does other things. "I keep the plot in my head when I'm running or swimming or biking. The story is there. I don't force myself to do anything except run it in my head."

This technique also works when he has a problem with the plot. "I take the focal point of what I'm stuck on and do something physical," says Chris. "It puts the problem in better perspective. Sometimes I do the opposite—unfocusing, meditating, listening to the rhythm of my running on the track. It lets me break loose." By the time he gets home, he usually has a number of possible solutions. "Usually one works."

Chris composes on a computer, which he loves. He even has a favorite key on the keyboard: the delete button. "You can be as stupid as you want to and no one will ever know." He rewrites a lot, and laughs with recognition at a comment by novelist Joseph Heller. Chris says it describes his own writing process as well: "Morning is throw-up time. Afternoon is cleanup time."

Getting his thoughts down on paper is most important. "The rest of the task is

sculpting, going back and shaping the story, throwing away what isn't working." The first few chapters usually need a lot of rewriting. "I'm still getting to know my characters at that point. I have to go back and make sure that the roundness of my characters and their dimensionality are as good in the beginning of the book as they are later."

After he finishes a novel he sometimes wants to write more about the characters. That's one reason he wrote his first book of short stories, *Athletic Shorts*, which features characters from his earlier books. He got

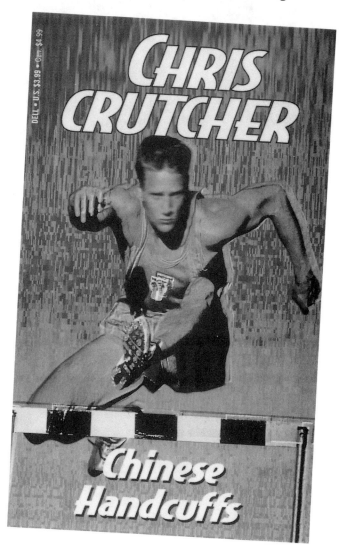

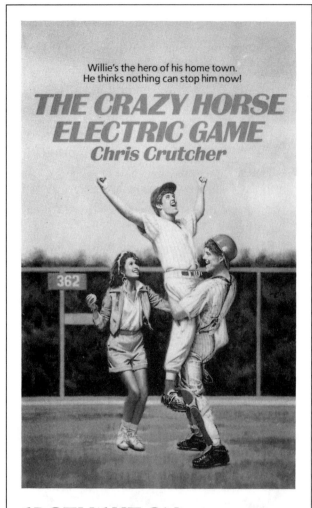

Willie's the hero of his home town.
He thinks nothing can stop him now!

# THE CRAZY HORSE ELECTRIC GAME
## Chris Crutcher

362

## SPOTLIGHT ON:
### THE CRAZY HORSE ELECTRIC GAME

Willie used to be on top of it all: a phenomenal athlete, the champ of the baseball team, and the hero of the Crazy Horse Electric game. But tragedy strikes and then seems to keep lumbering on, leaving Willie brain damaged from an accident. His speech is altered, as is his once glorious physical coordination. From inside his handicapped shell, Willie watches his family fall apart and his girlfriend date another boy. He fights to preserve the last "good" things in his life.

the idea while writing *Stoton*. "I needed one of the kids in the book to live alone," says Chris. "I thought of my character, Lionel. In one paragraph I described his parents as dying in an accident. It occurred to me that there had to be a story behind that." So he wrote a short story about how they died. From there, he realized there were advantages to writing about characters he already knew. "It tied together a lot of stuff."

Chris doesn't work from an outline. He never knows how the book will end until he's at least two-thirds of the way through. "When I'm writing the sixth or seventh chapter, the ending usually comes to me," he says. "That's when my writing becomes more focused, a lot leaner. When I write the first chapters, I'm still developing the characters."

Though his books are shelved in the young adult section, Chris doesn't see himself solely as a young adult novelist. "I may write about a seventeen-year-old, but whoever wants to read my book can read it." To create a teenage narrator, he goes back into his "fifteen- to twenty-one-year-old head."

> *"The word perfection was put on this planet to make us feel bad. Get rid of it. Delight in the stories you write."*

A death that takes place at the end of *Running Loose* was based on a tragedy that actually took place when Chris was twenty-one. As Chris wrote his book, he realized he was going to insert this sad memory into the story. But he didn't know how his characters were going to react to the development. As he reached that section in his manuscript, Chris remembers saying, "Watch this. Watch what happens," as if he were addressing one of the characters. After writing the scene, he went back to the beginning of the book to insert the hints or clues that indicate a tragic event will occur later on.

These days, he's writing a novel for adults that's set partly in the *Field of Dreams* of movie fame, which is now quite a tourist attraction in Dyersville, Iowa. Chris went to visit it last year. Soon after, he was talking with his mother about what Chris' father and her own father had been like at different stages in their lives. This gave Chris an idea. "I had a perfect image of traveling to the Field of Dreams, but instead of meeting all these baseball players, it's a vacant lot. You can see it, but it's snow-covered." The main character is thinly disguised as Chris, at his current age, forty-eight. At the Field of Dreams, he runs into his father and his maternal grandfather, both also forty-eight.

## LOOKING BACK

As a child, Chris loved to read biographies of famous people, especially sports heroes. He was fascinated with what the subjects were like as kids. "Then I got to junior high school and decided I was not going to do anything anybody wanted me to do," he remembers. Though he stopped reading, he was still interested in storytelling in general. "I was always in love with the plots from movies or television. I loved taking stories apart and wondering why the writers made the choices they did, why certain TV programs were funny and others that tried to be funny weren't."

## USEFUL SUGGESTIONS

Do you want to write? Here's Chris' advice. "Write all the time. Never listen to a voice that entered my head when I was writing *Running Loose*. It said, 'Who do you think you are? You're too big for your britches! You can't be famous!' Those thoughts could have stopped me from submitting that book. That voice comes from your childhood. Well-meaning people say things like that to keep you from getting hurt. You've got to trash them. You've got to turn your back on those words."

Chris hopes would-be writers understand that perfection is not a worthy goal. "The word perfection was put on this planet to make us feel bad," he says. "Get rid of it. Delight in the stories you write." ∎

# A WRITING ACTIVITY
## *from Chris Crutcher*

Write a story about a character in a convenience store. Have the character walk up and down the aisles, then leave without buying anything. The owner accuses him (or her) of stealing. What is the character's response? How does the character deal with the situation? Tell your tale!

# Paul Fleischman

**BORN:** September 5, 1952, in Monterey, California
**CURRENT HOME:** Pacific Grove, California

## SELECTED TITLES

**The Animal Hedge**
1983

**Path of the Pale Horse**
1983

**Finzel the Farsighted**
1983

**Coming-and-Going Men**
1985

**I Am Phoenix**
1985

**Rear-View Mirrors**
1986

**Rondo in C**
1988

**Joyful Noise**
1989

**Saturnalia**
1990

**Borning Room**
1991

**Bull Run**
1993

For Paul Fleischman, writing is like playing. "The whole way I go about writing a book is very close to the way I used to play with sticks and weeds and rocks and pine needles," he says. With those everyday objects, Paul would make "sound sculptures," arranging the pieces of found material so that they would twirl, click, and make noises.

"I also used to make little pine-needle houses when I was a student at Berkeley and was supposed to be doing more important things," he says. "Pine needles are very sharp, and they stick in well. People used to say that I was wasting time, but I'm absolutely serious when I say that I learned the principles of novel writing by making pine-needle houses. Building a book is like building anything. You have a notch, you have a slot, you put them together, and it feels good when it works."

Sometimes, it doesn't work. "Then there is a revision stage," says Paul, and for him this applies to any construction task. "Your sculpture might lean or not look good from all angles. Just as sculptors walk around their sculptures, I do the same when writing a book. I'm always walking around, looking at it, seeing what works and what doesn't work.

"So, the same principles are at work in playing and in writing: Experimentation, improvisation, creation, construction, deconstruction. In both processes, there is no one right answer." He loves that element of the unexpected that is part of both processes. "When you go up and down at the beach looking for driftwood, you don't know what you're going to find. You're just opening yourself to serendipity. Boy, without that I'd be dead. Serendipity is one of the writer's four food groups." (In case you're wondering, to Paul, the other three food groups are burritos, chocolate milk, and bagels.)

What happens when the task of construction and revision is complete? "Usually, there's a big pile of stuff left over that you didn't use. Most of my books have come out of that pile of scrap from earlier books, from things that didn't get used." Nothing is wasted.

Paul is often described as an innovator, which pleases him. "I'm proud of doing new books that haven't been done before," he says. It may be because he is the son of Sid Fleischman, himself a renowned children's book author. "I did not grow up with the intention of following in my father's footsteps," says Paul. "I wanted to do something different, as most kids would. But the older I got, the more I came to realize that what I was good at was writing children's books. Well, what was I going to do? One way to solve this problem was to do books that were different from those my father had done." Even this was tricky, because the two men have very similar interests. "We both like out-of-the-way corners of history. We both like to write in a rich style with lots of imagery." To create the necessary distance Paul needed to do his own original work, he listened hard to hear the voices inside his own imagination. "After I'd written *Graven Images* [1982], I realized I had found a style, a voice, I had been seeking for a long time. But I also realized it would only last me for a certain amount of time and then I would need to move on." That style lasted through his book *Coming-and-Going Men.* "As I was planning that book, I realized I'd been down this road too many times. New England, that same voice. I knew this was the last time I'd write in that style, at least for a while. There wasn't enough of a challenge anymore."

Challenge is what drives Paul. "When I walk upstairs to my

**WORDS FROM THE AUTHOR:**

*"I don't want to do a book that I've done before. Where's the challenge?"*

studio, there's always a little bit of sweat on the tips of my fingers. Will I pull it off? Is it worth doing? How's this scene going to go?" He's excited, apprehensive, nervous, and enthusiastic.

## THE WONDERFUL PORTABLE PENCIL

Paul writes his books in a spiral notebook, erasing and making changes as he goes along. "Word processors are great . . . for other people. The more thinking you do first, the less revising you do later. I think out my books in great detail first and take notes, so by the time I'm ready to write I know what I want to say. I write slowly, carefully, once!"

## A WRITING ACTIVITY
### from Paul Fleischman

I call this Story Forget. It's a good game, and it's very close to writing. I learned it from a friend who does improvisational theater. Here's how it goes: One person starts out by saying: "I was walking down the street when suddenly I stopped, and in front of me was a . . . . " Then that person stops. Somebody else has to fill in the line, by saying something like "Dinosaur!" Then the first person goes on from there. You don't have time to plan. The person telling the story has to continue to tell a plausible story.

He loves writing in pencil and says the pencil is a "wonderful, portable, versatile instrument. It's a fantastic tool that's completely overlooked. It has many, many advantages. You can write in a cabin in New Hampshire with no electricity. You can write on a plane, in a bus, wherever you are. I've written probably half my books in libraries. I just take my notebook along."

There's even a certain kind of library Paul prefers to write in: medical libraries. "The only people in there are snoring interns who have been up the night before. Snoring interns and me. *Path of the Pale Horse* was written in a medical library in Omaha, Nebraska. *Rear-view Mirrors* was written in a medical library at the University of New Mexico."

His writing room at home is spacious and uncluttered. "My desk is not the typical artist's messy desk." The room is full of light. "I live in a rather foggy place, so light is crucial." The room is quiet, too. "Those are the writer's other four food groups," says Paul, "space, orderliness, light, and quiet. I like quiet, because I'm saying those sentences over and over again all day."

Sounds, rather than pictures, are what matter to Paul when he writes, perhaps because he loves to listen to music, to perform it, and even to write it. "I often don't have a visual image of my characters in my head, I will admit. Maybe this is true of other authors, too. I've heard advice given to authors—to find a picture of somebody you imagine your character looking like and then tape it up. I don't do that."

Of course, he visualizes his stories' action in his head, which, he says, is one reason why he writes slowly, about a page a day. "Really the writer's main and hardest task is writing visual prose that will put that picture in somebody else's head." Sight is, Paul believes, our predominant sense. "That's why the Missouri license plate says 'The Show Me State' on it."

> *"The same principles are at work in playing and in writing: Experimentation, improvisation, creation, construction, deconstruction. In both processes, there is no one right answer."*

Paul is a patient writer, in spite of the relatively slow pace. "It doesn't bother me to write a page a day. A good, solid page is absolutely fine. I don't have too many morale problems. The only thing that depresses me is if the book isn't going well. But I've generally thought it out ahead of time."

If you think you want to be a writer, says Paul, "buy a notebook and save your ideas. I still have notebooks from when I was in high school more than twenty years ago. Save your ideas. You never know when you're going to need them. You'll be glad you wrote them down." Paul says he picks up ideas he wrote in his notebooks ten or fifteen years ago. ■

## SPOTLIGHT ON:
### JOYFUL NOISE

This funny and imaginative book of poems about insects is designed to be read aloud by two alternating voices. As you read the poems aloud, climb inside the insects' minds and see the world from their special points of view.

# Paula Fox

**BORN:** April 22, 1923, in New York, New York
**CURRENT HOME:** Brooklyn, New York

### SELECTED TITLES

**The Slave Dancer**
1975

**One-Eyed Cat**
1982

**A Place Apart**
1982

**A Likely Place**
1987

**Lily and the Lost Boy**
1987

**Portrait of Ivan**
1987

**The Stone-Faced Boy**
1987

**The Village by the Sea**
1988

**Maurice's Room**
1988

**Monkey Island**
1991

**The King's Falcon**
1992

**Amzat and His Brothers**
1993

**Western Wind**
1993

When Paula Fox is writing a book, it seems as though her mind never stops working. "It's as if there is some mobilization in my head. Everything I think becomes part of the process." She often carries a notebook around with her at those times. "If I have a thought, I put down a few words, because otherwise I'll lose it. I always have to write down things lest I lose them permanently."

Part of the reason thoughts fly away, she thinks, might be because "at my age it's ordinary to forget." But Paula also believes that the thoughts themselves are slippery little things. "You have to grab them, because they swim through your mind like fish in a tank. And then they're gone. Little silver fish, gone, gone." Sometimes the ideas flee before they're fully formed. "They don't have feet yet. They don't have legs. They don't walk. So I try to grab them while they're just a few words, so that I can remind myself." She compares capturing these unformed ideas to hooking onto the tip of an iceberg. "I write down the tip of the iceberg, so maybe I can haul out the iceberg later on."

Sometimes Paula's imagination reveals just the title of a story to her. She might not know what the title means. "After a while, maybe five years or maybe three months, I begin to see that there's something going on that I didn't know about."

For example, recently Paula was cleaning out some files. She found a little envelope marked "Dear Snake—Dear Rabbit." She also found a couple of pages of rough notes.

"The idea is that there is a correspondence between a boy and a girl and that something sinister happens," says Paula. As she looked at the words, ideas started to form. "I kept saying 'Dear Snake—Dear Rabbit.' The words began to shimmer in my mind. Gradually there are these strange streamers hanging from the words. I have to try to catch the streamers. Pretty soon, the idea begins to have some solidity."

## A MOBILE CHILDHOOD

Paula had an unusual childhood. Her father was a writer, and he and her mother moved around a lot. Paula did not always live with them. Her early years were spent living with a Congregational minister and his aged mother, in a big old house that overlooked New York's Hudson River. The minister, a writer himself, often read to her from his own work and talked to Paula about the difficulties of writing. Theirs was a house full of books. Paula remembers, "I learned to read when I was five, and I have been reading ever since. It seems to me to that it's the essential work of the writer."

The minister taught Paula the power of words—"that everything could count, that a word, spoken as meant, contained in itself an energy capable of awakening imagination, thought, and emotion."

Paula left the minister's house when she was about six years old. She lived

with her parents in California and then on a sugar plantation in Cuba. In Cuba, she attended a one-room schoolhouse and became fluent in Spanish. Later, she was taken to New York City. By the age of twelve, she had gone to nine schools. It was an unsettling childhood, one she is still trying to understand many years later through her writing.

Though Paula has chosen not to write her autobiography, she believes that in her books she tells her life's story in different ways. "The writer Albert Camus once said that there are two or three great images that come from one's childhood that one is always trying to evoke again, to understand them. It's a kind of explaining to yourself about your life."

*"Reading helps you think about things, it helps you imagine what it feels like to be somebody else . . . even somebody you don't like!"*

Sometimes Paula's readers will ask if a story is "made up." Paula says, "They think 'made up' means 'lying,' because they don't know about all those other things that go into writing." To those readers, Paula answers: "Everything is

ONE-EYED CAT
Paula Fox

## SPOTLIGHT ON:
### ONE-EYED CAT

A boy named Ned accidentally injures a stray cat with an air rifle. Ned is ashamed of his careless act but can't bring himself to admit he's done it. His guilt haunts him until he finally confesses to his mother. In turn, she makes a surprising confession of her own.

rooted in our lives, because we don't really know more than that." Each character in her books reflects her life's experiences, in ways she can't always explain. "I wasn't on a slave ship," she says, referring to *The Slave Dancer*. "I wasn't a boy who thought he shot a cat," referring to *The One-Eyed Cat*. "But those experiences are somehow rooted in my own sense of life, or how I see life, how I've experienced it."

## A RUMPLESTILTSKIN HOUSE

Paula lives in a "very funny sort of Rumplestiltskin house in Brooklyn" (New York). She describes the house as "very small but very tall." Her study is a twelve-by-twelve foot square room on the top floor. It has bookcases, a desk, a couch, and a pack of cards, "because I play solitaire a lot while I'm thinking."

She considers herself a visual writer. "I'd much rather read than be read to. I don't hear as well as I see. I have a sense of direction that makes people want to kill me, it's so good. I think it's because I see things and remember them. I don't see a road sign. I see a rock, or a strange roof, or a tree bent one way, and I remember it." The character Daniel, who appears at the end of the *Slave Dancer*, offers directions to two characters in the book the way Paula says she would do it: "Be careful of snakes. There's a turn in the road here and there's a funny tree there."

## SWIMMING IN A SEA OF RESEARCH

When Paula first got the idea for *The Slave Dancer*, she knew she had to do a lot of research to make the story come to life. She remembers going to the main public library in Brooklyn "where some nice person took me by the arm and shoved me toward a tremendous area of books on slavery. My heart sank. I didn't know how to do research. But I learned."

How did she know where to begin? She compares the process to moving to a new location. "I've moved a lot. When you first get in, and the moving men have left everything in a pile, you're horrified by the squalor of your possessions and the number of them. But after you put the first cinnamon can away, you're okay. It's just the first action that's hard."

In the case of research, she forced herself to open the first book. Then everything became possible. "It's like geometry," she says. "You have to pick a point. And it's not that you can find a beginning, because there is no beginning. From that first point, I went on. It's like crossing a stream on stepping stones. One step leads you to another."

She spent a year researching *The Slave Dancer.* "I had a tremendous stack of notes." Then when she began to write, she threw them away. "They were getting in my way. I was paralyzed with information."

All that research created in Paula a sensibility of the place and time. "At the beginning of the book, I wrote about a kerosene lamp. Then I stopped right in my tracks and thought, 'Were there kerosene lamps in New Orleans in 1840?' And there were not. You're not aware of how much you take in." She took the lamp out and proceeded with her writing.

## YESTERDAY AND TODAY

Sometimes Paula thinks of how different today's world is from that in which she grew up. "When I was young, things were much more clearly defined than they are today. There were very clear villains, like Hitler and the Depression." These days, she feels, young people have to cope with a world "without sharp, restful

lines. Children sprawl all over the place. They can never rest in the arms of authority."

In her mind, the influence of television is partly to blame. "One of the terrible things about television is that it's taken local life away from children. When I was little, you mooched around. You got lost in the woods. You found a snake. You got into a little trouble. Now, your backyard is television. Television is so narrow and banal and stupid most of the time and addictive. It's everybody's backyard. When I was a kid, the idea was not to be like other kids. Now everybody's supposed to be the same."

What does Paula Fox wish kids would do instead? Read. "When you begin to read, read everything. Reading helps you think about things, it helps you imagine what it feels like to be somebody else . . . even somebody you don't like!" ∎

## A WRITING ACTIVITY
### from Paula Fox

Imagine a room that contains a table with a checkered cloth on it. On the table is a can of evaporated milk. Write about the people who live in that room. What do they look like? What are their likes and dislikes? What are they trying to achieve?

# S. E. Hinton

**BORN:** 1950 in Tulsa, Oklahoma
**CURRENT HOME:** Tulsa, Oklahoma

With each of her books, S(usan) E(loise) Hinton has used a different approach to composing. "I've tried going from a real short draft to a real long draft. That was *The Outsiders*. I tried writing slowly and carefully— two pages a day—until the book was done. That was *That Was Then . . . This Is Now*. I once wrote a short story that grew into a novel. That was *Rumble Fish*. I've also written a complete book from a partial outline. That was *Tex*. One time, I wrote a novel from a complete outline. That was *Taming the Star Runner*. I keep looking for the magic process to make it easy," Susan says. "I haven't found it yet, but I keep trying."

A writer since third grade, she has always liked making up stories and molding the endings to her liking. An avid horseback rider, she especially loved writing horse stories. Which book is her favorite? Marguerite Henry's *King of the Wind*. "I still reread that every year," she says. In sixth grade she even taught herself to type "so my stories would look more professional."

It's no surprise, then, that Susan's writing career got an early start. At age fifteen she began writing *The Outsiders*, and by age eighteen, just as she began college, it was published to rave reviews. Had Susan been an extrovert, going on publicity tours and being interviewed would have been a thrill. But Susan was shy and felt uncomfortable around adults. During one of her early interviews, she said: "I do the best I can, but sometimes I wish I'd never written the thing. Then I remember why I wrote it and I don't mind so much."

She wrote *The Outsiders* because a friend of hers got beaten up. "I wanted to do something that would change people's opinion of greasers." ( In Hinton's school "Greasers" were poorer kids who tended to act tough and grease their hair back.) "Some 'socs' [the abbreviation of socials, that school's crowd of more well-to-do kids] didn't like the way my friend was combing his hair, so they beat him up. Another

## SELECTED TITLES

**The Outsiders**
1967

**That Was Then . . . This Is Now**
1971

**Rumble Fish**
1975

**Taming the Star Runner**
1988

**Tex**
1989

**Big David, Little David**
1994

**The Puppy Sister**
1995

friend of mine never got enough to eat and frequently slept in the bus station because his father was always beating him up. The socs teased him because of his grades. Grades!"

With the success of *The Outsiders*, Susan realized she had found a subject that was important to her: teenagers struggling to grow up. But the attention the book attracted made Susan scared to write again. What if its popularity had been a fluke? For a while, she felt paralyzed. Before long, though, she started writing again—slowly, one or two pages a day. Four years later *That Was Then . . . This Is Now* was published.

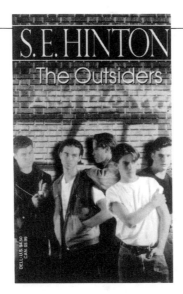

## HOLLYWOOD KNOCKS

Four of Susan's books have been made into films: *Tex, Rumble Fish, That Was Then . . . This Is Now* and *The Outsiders*. Oftentimes, when a book is made into a film, the book's author is not included in the process. Susan's experience was different: she collaborated on two of the screenplays and was a creative consultant on a third.

How does novel writing compare to screen writing? "When you're writing a novel, you're in total control, which can be wonderful but scary. You've got to include everything," she points out. "But in screen writing, there's so much collaboration."

Susan considers herself lucky. "I enjoyed my collaborators very much. It's a lot of fun if you do it with the right people." Novel writing can be lonely. "It's ten times more fun to work on a screenplay than it is to shut yourself up in a room with a legal pad. There's much more energy. It bounces off everybody."

Fortunately, Susan worked with open-minded directors. "They were happy to take ideas from wherever they came," she says. "They didn't need total control. If a suggestion worked, the director would accept it. It opened me up to collaboration." Working on the screenplays was so much fun, Susan admits that afterwards, it was a hard to go back to her "four walls," to work in a room by herself.

Screen writing is easier than book writing, says Susan. "You can buy a book about screen writing format in a store. Once you've watched a movie being put together, it's easier to write a screenplay." The experience of working on a movie set has expanded her horizons greatly. "I lived on a movie set for two years straight. I've learned that you've got to keep things moving in a screenplay. You've got to make it visual. You can't have speeches two or three sentences long. I happen to be really good at writing dialogue. That's been a big plus in my work."

---

## WORDS FROM THE AUTHOR:

*"I sometimes dream about the characters in my books. Not the actors, but the ones I always saw when I was writing."*

## ALWAYS WORKING

Is there one best place to write? "I keep looking for the right spot," Susan says. When she wrote *The Outsiders*, she took the manuscript with her everywhere. "I wrote at school, at home, at Thanksgiving dinner. I'd drag that thing around with me wherever I went. I had extreme powers of concentration."

*That Was Then* . . . was written as she sat at the kitchen table, her cat in her lap. *Rumble Fish* was also composed in a kitchen, this one in California. "My husband was at graduate school. Every Friday night he'd play poker until three in the morning. That's when I'd sit down at the kitchen island and write." What about *Tex*? "Written on top of a rolltop desk."

"*Tex* was a miserable book to write, though I'm happy with how it came out," Susan laughs. "Part of that time the air conditioning was out. And I had writer's block." The book took a long time to write—about three and a half years. At the time she was also working eight to twelve hours every day in a shoe store. (She and her husband opened the first Earth Shoe store in Tulsa.) "I couldn't figure out why I

## SPOTLIGHT ON:
### *RUMBLE FISH*

Which of Susan's Books does she wish her readers knew better? "*Rumble Fish*. It is my easiest book to read but the hardest to understand. It's about myth making, and the need for folk heroes. A lot of people don't define their terms when they set out to make a hero out of someone. The book was written to point out the dangers of identifying too strongly with someone before you know what kind of person he really is."

wasn't getting any writing done."

Plotting that book was hard. "About fifty pages had gone off on a tangent, sending the book in a direction it wasn't supposed to go. When rereading my manuscript, I finally forced myself to realize what I had done. I'd tear up the pages and put things away for a month at a time and not look at them." She'd usually get back on track thanks to "an inspiration from weird sources," such a newspaper article she had read.

Upon completing *Tex*, Susan spent the next few years working on the movies. Then she and her husband had a son. "I decided I wasn't going to think about teenagers for a while. I was going to think about babies," says Susan. When her son turned four and started preschool, she rented an office on the same block as his preschool and wrote *Taming the Star Runner*. "I had the outline on paper for many years."

Did she mind giving up her writing during the baby's infancy? "I didn't mind the hiatus," she says. "I was real happy with my baby. I was so thrilled. I knew I'd get back to writing, but he wasn't ever going to be a baby again."

## CHARACTER IS EVERYTHING

How do Susan's books usually form in her mind? "I always start with characters. Everything comes out of them," she says.

Susan finds the beginnings of her books easy to write. "My characters and their goals set up the setting. That's why I find the first chapter the easiest to write." Endings are usually clear to her from the outset, as well. "I could write the last sentence first." It's "the muddle in the middle" that's the hardest for her to write.

## HER SPECIAL AUDIENCE

"Teenagers take things really seriously," says Susan. "That's one reason I stuck with the genre for so long. Even among the roughest ones they've still got a funny, idealistic streak." She sees the teenage years as ones when "your ideals are bouncing up against a wall of compromise. It's a bloody battle."

*"I always start with characters. Everything comes out of them."*

The "uniforms" of teenagers have changed over the years, Susan observes, but their feelings haven't altered at all. She can still remember how she felt at that age, which helps her "voice" stay true. "I was very eccentric. I was a tomboy, doing a lot of guy stuff. Most of my close friends were guys. That's why I write from a boy's point of view. As it turns out, a boy's point of view is easiest for me, so I've stuck with it."

## A WRITING ACTIVITY
### from S. E. Hinton

Tell a story from an inanimate object's point of view. What does it see? What would it say about the people and other objects in its surroundings? If you're stuck for ideas, start with a television set, which may begin: "They watch me all day, but do they know I watch them? This is what goes on."

If you want to be a writer, Susan suggests that you read everything you can. "That way you know you're not going to have to sit down and study what makes a sentence, how to make a paragraph, and all that structure stuff. It will just be in your subconscious. Just make your characters speak. The technicalities will be there in your subconscious, where you don't have to mess with them. It's scary enough just sitting down and trying to write, without trying to remember what the rules of composition are."

As for teachers of writing: "If you're trying to teach the rules of composition, that's what you should teach. If you're trying to teach how to enjoy writing, let the kids experiment and do things that may not be correct—let them find their strengths. Don't give somebody an F because of a misspelled word. Circle it, hand it back and say 'correct your spelling.' That's what an editor is going to do, not flunk you. If you want to be a writer, you have to love writing. It gets hard later on. You have to start out by liking it." ■

# Will Hobbs

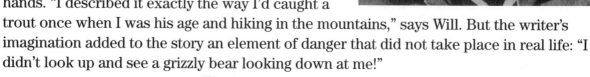

**BORN:** August 22, 1947, in Pittsburgh, Pennsylvania
**CURRENT HOME:** Durango, Colorado

In everything he writes, Will Hobbs draws from his own experiences. "Hiking in the mountains, white-water rafting, working with sea turtles—all of these are things I do myself." Most of the incidents in his books grow from his imagination, as he thinks of characters having adventures in places he knows and loves.

For example, in Will's book *Bearstone*, the character Cloyd catches a fish with his bare hands. "I described it exactly the way I'd caught a trout once when I was his age and hiking in the mountains," says Will. But the writer's imagination added to the story an element of danger that did not take place in real life: "I didn't look up and see a grizzly bear looking down at me!"

## SELECTED TITLES

**Changes in Latitudes**
1988

**Bearstone**
1989

**Downriver**
1991

**The Big Wander**
1992

**Beardance**
1993

**Kokopelli's Flute**
1995

**Beardream**
1996

The book *Downriver*, largely set on the Colorado River as it winds through the Grand Canyon, contains a number of incidents from Will's many runs through the canyon in his own white-water raft. "The flash-flood scene, for example," says Will. "And on one of our trips, my brother-in-law brought a live scorpion into camp in a blue plastic soap dish. In the story, one of the characters slips the soap dish into his back pocket and declares, 'Live scorpion in pants makes life interesting.'"

Some of Will's characters are completely made up. Others are based, in part, on traits of people he has known. But once he begins writing, the characters come to life. "The characters are speaking and acting, taking on a life of their own, and my fingers are *flying*, just trying to keep up."

## THE IMPORTANCE OF LANDSCAPE

Will considers landscape to be as important to his stories as any of the characters. "I was exploring the places in the novels years before I started writing. I keep going back now for inspiration—on real trips and in journeys of the imagination as I work." He writes about his favorite places to share them with his readers, hoping that they'll go away with "what's often called *spirit of place.*"

He dedicated his book *Downriver* to David Brower, a conservationist, whom Will says is the living person he most admires. "He's dedicated his life to saving wild places. It was his leadership in the 1960s, when he led the Sierra Club, that prevented two dams and reservoirs from being built in the Grand Canyon." Will admires many of the other leaders in the conservation movement, as well. "I believe they are playing a vital role in preserving what can still be saved in the natural world. It's an uphill fight all the way. I hope it's an effort today's kids will want to participate in."

## A WRITING "NEST"

Will and his wife Jean live in southwestern Colorado, about eighteen miles outside the town of Durango. They live in a house Will built himself, "from the foundation up," over a period of ten years. Will's study is on the second floor, looking out on pine trees and "usually, the blue Colorado sky." Over his desk is a bulletin board full of photographs of family members and special places. There's also a painting a reader sent him "of sea turtles swimming in a night sky," called "Navigating by the Stars." This art

High on a Mountain, Lone Bear Discovers the Power of His Brave Heritage
**BEARSTONE**
AWARD-WINNING AUTHOR
**WILL HOBBS**
An ALA Best Book
AVON CAMELOT
$3.50 U.S.
$4.50 CAN.

was influenced by Will's book *Changes in Latitudes.*

The writer's desk is arrayed with "a number of totems," such as a few small river rocks, a wind-up pterodactyl, a blue bearstone, and a turtle fetish made for him by a reader. "It's my writing 'nest' and makes me feel right as I face the blank screen of the word processor," he says.

Each time he gets ready to write, Will undertakes a ritual. He exercises, showers, then procrastinates. When he can delay no longer, he sits down to work. "I have a deal with myself," he says. "I wind up the little pterodactyl. When the pterodactyl walks, I have to start writing something, anything." He finds that after a few minutes, he's engaged, and he can keep writing. He's even having fun, and wonders, "Why did it take me so long to get started?"

## GETTING UNDERWAY

Sometimes the idea for a book comes from a single image. For example, Will began writing *The Big Wander*, set in and around Monument Valley, Utah, with the

## WORDS FROM THE AUTHOR:

*"Write with the five senses. That's how you make your writing come alive for the reader."*

image of a boy leading a burro into the canyon country to the west of the valley. Later, he combined that image with a quote from Aldo Leopold, a famous naturalist: "I am glad I shall never be young without wild country to be young in. Of what avail are forty freedoms without a blank spot on the map?"

Will had hiked in that "blank spot" many times before. Now, with the image of the boy and the burro in his mind, he returned to Monument Valley, then hiked into the canyon of the Escalante River. As he hiked, he soaked up fresh impressions of this beautiful, mysterious area.

After the hiking trip, Will returned home and read about the area. "I read about Navajos and Mormons. I read books about burros, books about the flooding of Glen Canyon." As he thumbed through one of the burro

books, he saw a photograph of an old-timer in a parade in Flagstaff, Arizona. "He was walking down the street with a backpack on his back. Sticking out of that backpack was the head and improbably large ears of a live baby burro. Bingo! I knew I had to have that image in my story."

*"When you're writing from a young person's point of view, you're in the realm of hope and possibility. That's a good place to be."*

As he did his background reading, Will took notes about possible characters and plots. He follows this procedure with each book he writes. His impressions of what he will write changes as he does his research. Most of what he reads never shows up in the novel. Much of what he originally thought the story would be about doesn't show up, either. "But in all that confusion there are those certain powerful images that I know have to wind up in the story."

His book *Changes in Latitudes* began with a single image, as well—the image of somebody swimming along with sea turtles. *Beardance* began with the image of a boy denning with bears. "The rest of the process is a journey of discovery—how to make it happen."

Will has learned over the years, that his first draft is "merely an attempt to get something going." He's always written at least three drafts of each novel—though he wrote six for *Bearstone* (actually his

## A WRITING ACTIVITY
### from Will Hobbs

Think of a natural setting that you feel very strongly about—a lake, a pond, a meadow, a mountainside, a spot in a city park. Visit it in person or in your memory, and make a list of impressions that come from your five senses.

Now, think of an animal that lives in the special place. Write a story in which you or your character *is changed in some way* through an encouter with the creature.

first novel, though it was the second to be published). He starts each new draft fresh. He does not cut and paste from a former draft.

With each new novel, Will finds he has a new problem to solve. With *Downriver*, Will's problem was finding the right voice. "The first three drafts are each told by a different first-person narrator," says Will. "The first two narrators I tried didn't even end up in the final group of seven kids who ran the river."

## A MOVING CHILDHOOD

Will grew up in a family of five children, four boys and a girl. (He's in the middle.) His father was in the Air Force, so they moved all over. They lived in Alaska for a while, where Will "fell in love with mountains and rivers." When they lived in California, Will loved running up into the hills every day after school—to explore. "I liked to catch lizards in a noose fashioned from a wild oat shoot and then let them go." He was also a big fan of baseball, fishing, and gardening with his dad.

Will did not enjoy having to be the "new kid" so many times in his childhood, but he liked school. He had a lot of good teachers, and he liked to read. "I read tons of novels—outdoor adventures, animal stories, and

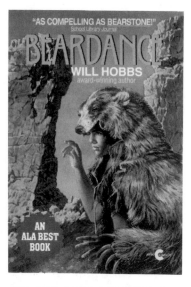

## SPOTLIGHT ON: *BEARDANCE*

Cloyd Atcitty witnesses the tragic death of a mother grizzly and soon finds himself risking his own life to rescue her helpless cubs. To do so, Cloyd must protect them from nature (the mountain's deadly winter) and man (trophy hunters).

mysteries." He also remembers reading "a whole shelf of biographies written like novels."

He didn't write very much when he was young. "It was more like a secret dream I had." Back then, he just assumed it was necessary to have some kind of extraordinary talent to actually write stories yourself. He first tested his wings as a writer when he was in college. He's glad that schools today emphasize writing more. "Kids are growing up thinking of themselves as readers *and* writers."

## HOPE AND POSSIBILITY

A former seventh- and eighth-grade reading and English teacher, Will likes writing children's books, because "when you're writing from a young person's point of view, you're in the realm of hope and possibility. That's a good place to be."

He wants his readers to take away from his books "a sense of adventure about life, a sense of wonder, a sense of hope." He feels that many of his readers are struggling with the difficult job of growing up. "Lots of them are struggling. Many have been dealt a difficult hand. Lots have made bad decisions already in their lives." But he believes in the power of the individual, to dream and to hope. "You can build on your strengths and your good choices." ∎

# M. E. Kerr

**BORN:** May 27, 1927, in Auburn, New York
**CURRENT HOME:** East Hampton, New York

## SELECTED TITLES

**Dinky Hocker Shoots Smack**
1972

**Him She Loves?**
1984

**I Stay Near You**
1985

**Night Kites**
1986

**Fell**
1987

**Fell Back**
1989

**The Son of Someone Famous**
1991

**What I Really Think of You**
1991

**Fell in Love**
1992

**Fell Down**
1993

**Linger**
1993

**Deliver Us from Evie**
1994

M. E. Kerr (Marijane Meaker) sometimes bases the characters in her books on people she meets in real life. There is one person, a child, who M. E. Kerr remembers in particular. "I was in a park. There I saw a kid standing in front of her father's van—the family were religious fundamentalists—which had a big loudspeaker on the roof. Evidently, the girl's father was making her hand out leaflets for a 'Twenty-four Hour Prayer Soaking.' This kid's face was down to her shoes. She was such a sad, vulnerable little kid. The high school kids nearby were making fun of her. The poor girl was in agony." Kerr, whose real name is Marijane Meaker, took home the memory of that child. The youngster became the model for the character Opal Ringer in *What I Really Think of You*.

"I saw her eyes and her face as I was writing that book," says Marijane. Curious about the lives of religious fundamentalists, she "visited the church several times." While there, Marijane avoided identifying herself as a writer. She's sure that would have changed the way the people in the church behaved around her. "It would have made them uncomfortable."

An interest in current events and her own observations have inspired many of Marijane's books. *Linger* was written as a reaction to television coverage of the 1991 Gulf War. "Television didn't tell the whole story," she says unhappily. "We didn't see people being killed. All we saw were fireworks, nothing more. It was a very controlled presentation by the press. Nobody dead. No dead anything."

This troubled Marijane. "I lived through Vietnam on television," she says, recalling the horrifying scenes of war that were displayed on nightly television. "I knew we weren't getting the whole story on the Gulf War." She thinks that the government was careful not to anger people about the recent war because many had become angry about Vietnam. "This time there was censorship. Everybody was aware of it except for young kids."

## "I often think about the world's problems and how they affect children."

Then the local newspaper ran an article about a Gulf War soldier who was badly injured by friendly fire—an accidental shelling from an American tank. "That inspired me to do this book. I had thought throughout the Gulf War that this is a war our kids have lived through. They're old enough to remember the yellow ribbons and the American flags. But I realized that if they do remember it, it will be as something that happened overnight and didn't hurt anybody. Maybe they would grow up to think of war as the easy way out of a situation. I wanted to dramatize it a little more."

*Linger* focuses on a correspondence between a Gulf War soldier and a girl back home. "I often think about the world's problems, and how they affect children," says Marijane. "It's incredible to me what kids know now about violence and about diseases such as AIDS. Subjects are brought right into the

classroom that we were slow to learn about." Marijane believes that even though kids know about difficult subjects, they don't necessarily understand them. She hopes her books help kids put the issues into perspective.

Marijane's house is a gathering place for many teenagers from the neighborhood, though she has no children of her own. "I love having them here," she says. "They listen to me, which they don't always do elsewhere. They respect my privacy. I have a stuffed rabbit. I hang it on the door. If it's there, they don't come in." When the neighborhood kids visit, they often bring

M. E. KERR
Best-selling author of *Gentlehands*

Was the real danger in the Persian Gulf . . . or at home?

LINGER

PROPRIETOR NED DUNLINGER ~ ESTABLISHED 19

## SPOTLIGHT ON:
### *FELL DOWN*

This story is told by Fell and a ventriloquist's alter ego, his dummy. Fell drops out of prep school, but is drawn back, into a mystery of kidnapping, murder, disguise, and obsession. Students will enjoy how the two stories come together.

over their tapes and CDs, which Marijane loves, since she's a big fan of rock music. "I love knowing them," she says. "I know the best parts of them, in a way. I'm distanced from them."

## EARLY YEARS

Who influenced Marijane as a child? Her father taught her to be a great reader. "He was a mayonnaise manufacturer, with a strange habit, for a mayonnaise manufacturer, of reading everything . . ."

Many teachers along the way encouraged Marijane's interest in both reading and writing. But her greatest influence, she is convinced, was her mother, whom Marijane says was a "world" class gossip . . . One of the most vivid memories of my childhood is of my mother making a phone call. First, she'd tell me to go out and play. I'd pretend to do that, letting the back door slam, hiding right around the corner of the living room, in the hall. She'd have her pack of Kools and the ashtray on the desk, as she gave the number of one of her girlfriends to the operator . . . My mother would begin nearly every conversation the same way, 'Wait till you hear this!'" Of her mother's style as a storyteller, which she has inherited, Marijane says: "She never just blurted it out. She filled in all the background. Great suspense. She was a natural raconteur."

## MANY IDENTITIES

When she is interviewed, Marijane is usually asked about her many pseudonyms. She began her writing career as a teenager in the 1940s. Writing under the name Eric Rantham McKay, she sent out stories to many magazines, all of which were rejected. "They came back like boomerangs, with printed rejection slips attached. But sometimes these rejection slips had a 'sorry' penciled across them, or 'try again.'" Marijane cherished these bits of encouragement and used them to lift her spirits as she began a new piece.

After college, Marijane moved to New York City. After a brief career in publishing, she began to write full-time. She wrote under many names, including Laura Winston, Mamie Stone, Edgar Stone, and Winston Albert. It was "Laura Winston" who made Marijane's first sale, in 1951. Her writing career had finally begun.

Marijane lists two reasons for her many pseudonyms. First, she simply likes the idea of naming herself. Second, she has always been a prolific writer. She worries that she would compete against herself if she tried to publish too many works under her own name.

In the 1950s and 1960s, she wrote mystery novels under the name Vin Packer. Why Vin Packer? Her editor thought that Marijane's writing style was "fast and tough." He thought she would lose credibility with a name like Marijane Meaker. Since she was already an old hand at changing her name, she combined the first and last name of two friends and changed her identity once again.

She wrote books in the early 1960s under her own name, and that of M. J. Meaker. Her friend, the late writer Louise Fitzhugh, author of *Harriet the Spy*, urged Marijane to take a look at the young adult market. "I started looking over the field," says Marijane. "I came across *Pigman* by Paul Zindel. He gave me the inspiration to write a book for kids without stooping. Just a book from the heart, without trying to cater to kids or to get to their level. Before, I always worried about vocabulary, and how to talk like a child. Paul's book helped me see that you don't have to do any of that. You just have to tell a good story." Finally, in 1968, the writer M. E. Kerr published her first book, *Dinky Hocker Shoots Smack*. And a whole new career for Marijane began.

Today, Marijane lives in the country, where she enjoys cooking, visiting friends, and listening to rock music. She continues to write, this time dabbling in the genre of fantasy. Writing for a younger audience, she uses the pseudonym Mary James. "She is my latest disguise," says Marijane cheerfully. ∎

## A WRITING ACTIVITY
### from M. E. Kerr

The opening line of anything you write is very important. Think of a subject you care about. Now write down three good ways to start the piece ("leads"). Read them over. Read them to a classmate. Which one grabs your readers by the collar and says: "Listen!"? With this good opening, continue the rest of the piece.

# Julius Lester

**BORN:** January 27, 1939, in St. Louis, Missouri
**CURRENT HOME:** Amherst, Massachusetts

## SELECTED TITLES

**Black Folktales**
1970

**This Strange New Feeling**
1982

**The Knee-High Man and Other Tales**
1985

**To Be a Slave**
1986

**The Tales of Uncle Remus**
1987

**Long Journey Home**
1988

**Lovesong: Becoming a Jew**
(autobiographical)
1988

**How Many Spots Does a Leopard Have? and Other Tales**
1989

**The Last Tales of Uncle Remus**
1994

Julius Lester has many identities: professor, musician, singer, and writer. Moving between these separate selves lets him enjoy the best of what each has to offer. "My identity has never been focused solely on my writing," Lester says. "Writing is something I do and love and can't imagine living without, but my ego is not involved with being a writer. Writing is an expression of myself. When a student comes to me and says 'I want to be a writer,' I say, 'that's fine. What do you want to write?'"

Lester believes that to call yourself a writer is to make a claim on a social identity. But to actually *be* a writer is to make a decision to "devote your life's energy to the process, to center your life around it in many ways."

## EARLY YEARS

As a black child growing up in the American South during the 1940s and 1950s, he experienced firsthand a great deal of segregation and discrimination. He remembers that in his adolescent years, the South forced "many restrictions on where [blacks] could live, eat, go to school, and go after dark."

As an escape, Lester read. The books helped him understand "that the segregated world in which I was forced to live . . . was not the only reality. Somewhere beyond that world, somewhere my eyes could not then penetrate, were dreams and possibilities, and I knew this was true because the books I read ravenously, desperately, were voices from that world."

## WORKING FOR CHANGE

In college, Lester was active in the civil rights movement. After he graduated, he moved to New York City and got involved in folk singing. He went back to the South periodically, becoming a leader in an organization called the Student Nonviolent Coordinating Committee. He also became a professional folk singer, recording two albums. He performed with many well-kown singers, such as Pete Seeger, Phil Ochs, and Judy Collins.

Over the next few years, Lester continued to express himself in many ways. He began to write books, for adults at first.

He also became a radio announcer, introducing his audiences to the wide variety of music that interested him. This was important to him, for through that instrument he could be a "voice" that entered people's houses and apartments, keeping them company. His fans often wonder if there were tapes made of his radio programs. There were not. "I felt I

Six true stories of freedom by the author of *To Be a Slave*, a Newbery Honor Book

**WORDS FROM THE AUTHOR:**

*"I love teaching. I love students. I was born to teach."*

was creating in time and space, and that it wasn't supposed to be preserved. If it *was* going to be preserved, it would be preserved in the hearts and minds of people. And that's what happened."

One day an editor suggested he try writing for children. He responded by producing *To Be a Slave*, which used the actual words of former-slaves to tell their story. More than twenty-five years later, this classic is still read widely. And with its success, Lester found another avenue for expression.

## WRITING THE TRUTH

Currently, Lester is a university professor who helps his students "find themselves" by understanding religion. He still sings, although folk songs take a smaller role in his life than years ago. Since his conversion to Judaism in the 1980s, he has served as a cantor, singing and chanting religious music and helping lead the congregation in prayer. And his writer's "self" is very active.

"I like writing for kids," he says. "I suppose the main reason is that I can write more honestly for them than I can for adults. When I write for adults, I'm judged on my literary technique. I'm compared with this person and that person. That's not why I write. I want to tell a story, to join with the person who's reading it. I want my story to join their story."

> "Regardless of what I'm teaching, what my students want to know from me is how to be in the world, with the fullness of being."

Lester writes in a large room that looks out over hills. "It's quiet," he says thoughtfully. His walls are full of images he likes to look at, which change from time to time. These days, the images are of Israel, of the Western Wall in Jerusalem, of wolves, and of a snake. Above his desk, he posts lines that have come to him from dreams over the years. "I put them up to remember the mysteries of these different things."

Which great thinkers have influenced Lester over the years? He points to the psychiatrist Carl Jung, who wrote about dreams and their relationship to the unconscious mind. Lester ponders Jung's message: We are thinking all the time, Jung believed, though we are not always aware of all of our thoughts, because

Scholastic 0-590-42460-2 / $3.25 US / $3.95 CAN

point

TO BE A SLAVE

Julius Lester
A Newbery Honor Book

## SPOTLIGHT ON:
### TO BE A SLAVE

This collection of six stories is based on first-hand accounts of former slaves. Readers have the extraordinary experience of understanding what it was like to live under the terrible circumstances of slavery. Lester has called this type of book "history from the ground up."

they take place in our unconscious. To tap into this thought stream, Jung believed, it is necessary to pay close attention to your dreams.

"I learned through Jung that the aim is to keep your conscious and unconscious minds very close together," says Lester. "If they get split apart, we have problems. If we keep them close together, all kinds of wonderful things can happen."

Astrology also holds interest for Lester. "Astrology has been extremely important in my life in terms of helping me to see myself and to accept myself." His current project is a book for young adults. "It's about astrology. I'll tell the myths behind each sign," Lester says.

## KIDS' PROBLEMS

Lester thinks about how hard it is to grow up, especially today. "I think one of the biggest problems facing children today is that adults, for the most part, are not very good role models. I don't think adults really present children with a vision of what it means to be human, and all the possibilities involved." He's afraid that kids will grow up with a limited sense of their possibilities. "They're experiencing a lot of fear. At the present time, adults are not doing a very good job of being adults."

Lester thinks too about his students. "Regardless of what I am teaching, what my students want to know from me is

*point*

THIS STRANGE NEW FEELING

Scholastic 0-590-44647-0 | $2.75 US  $3.95 CAN

*Julius Lester*

how to be in the world, with the fullness of being. They want to know how I did it. How I did it may not be how they will do it, but at least they need to know it's possible—that one person did it."

As a teacher and as a writer, Lester hopes to show that each of us is important. "I try to convey that everyday life is to be valued, and that each person is of value. If you struggle to live your life with as much integrity as you can muster, that is heroic. You don't have to do 'great things' or be on television to be a person of value." Lester believes that one of the functions of literature is to tell people that they have worth. "I do that by telling stories." ■

## A WRITING ACTIVITY
### from Julius Lester

Keep a journal. Put in there what happens to you day by day, and you'll have an incredible record. I've kept a journal on and off since I was fifteen. It's an amazing document. In addition, through journal-writing you learn unconsciously how to put words together.

# Janet Taylor Lisle

**BORN:** February 13, 1947, in Englewood, New Jersey
**CURRENT HOME:** Little Compton, Rhode Island

As a child, Janet Taylor Lisle always wondered about the existence of fairies. "I saw small bits of evidence around," she says. "I was very much on the lookout and very aware that other worlds were operating, secretly, when I was a small child." To her, clues were everywhere. "I would see berries sprinkled around on the terrace and think someone had been there. I would detect small footprints and know that magic beings had come during the night."

### SELECTED TITLES

**The Dancing Cats of Applesap**
1985

**Sirens and Spies**
1985

**The Great Dimpole Oak**
1987

**Afternoon of the Elves**
1989

**The Lampfish of Twill**
1993

**Forest**
1993

**The Gold Dust Letters**
1994

**Looking for Juliette**
1994

She wrote letters to fairies, too, and was delighted to get responses, though she later learned that a loved one was leaving the letters for her. (Her recent book, *The Gold Dust Letters*, is based, in part, on this memory.) When she received the letters, Janet thought she was communicating with "another world that was just slightly beyond the rim, just beyond my sight. I could see evidence of it, and I could hear it too, buzzings and clickings."

For example, she suspected that just such odd sounds, coming regularly from beneath her family's summer house, had supernatural origins. "I would listen to them and think that there was some strange world under there that I would like to see. But I couldn't quite see it, hidden away in the shadows. Of course, I imagined all sorts of things." Years later, she realized that the sounds were caused by vibrations the family washing machine made in the kitchen under the house.

Janet still believes that magic operates in our world. "Mysteries exist, just offstage, just beyond our understanding." She compares her curiosity about the unknown to that of scientists, who are "involved in the process of discovering the subatomic world, the universe, of trying to assimilate pieces of information." In science, as in her own imaginative life, Janet thinks there is always a moment when "the mystery that seemed so impossible to understand is revealed." This curiosity about the world and its workings seems to Janet to be very human. "And it hardly matters whether you're four or five, or fifty or sixty." But children seem to specialize in using their imaginations to come up with explanations. "That's why children are so wonderful to write for," says Janet. "They are completely and unselfconsciously inventive."

## WRITING FROM THE INSIDE OUT

Ideas, rather than experiences, are at the center of Janet's writing. "I don't have an overwhelming experience and then race upstairs to my writing room." Instead, as she works out her stories, "various notions I have about the world, or about people, or things I read in the newspaper, come weaving in."

An issue that runs through Janet's writing is perception, the way different people look at the same thing. One of her early books, *The Great Dimpole Oak*, is about a tree that is important to many people in many different ways. "I just planted that tree right in the middle of the book," she says. "I was very interested in how it was going to be

viewed by various characters around the outside. As I wrote, I inhabited each of these characters and then plotted what my reaction would be. How would I see this tree? How would this tree change by my looking at it?"

*Afternoon of the Elves* is about various points of view, too. In that book, a lonely girl, Sara-Kate, invites a neighbor girl, Hillary, to share a secret: a tiny village in her backyard made entirely of sticks, twigs, and stones. Sara-Kate insists that the village was built by elves. Hillary doesn't know whether to believe her or not. "The elf village is open to interpretation, just like the *Great Dimpole Oak*," says Janet.

Janet's readers ask her repeatedly whether the village is real. They are upset when she can't give them a clear answer. "They think that since I am the

## WORDS FROM THE AUTHOR:

*"In a way, the best writers for children are those who are best at convincing kids that we are with them, that we are writing from their side, not presenting them with a platter full of proper ways to be, or correct ways to live, how to grow up right or improve themselves."*

53

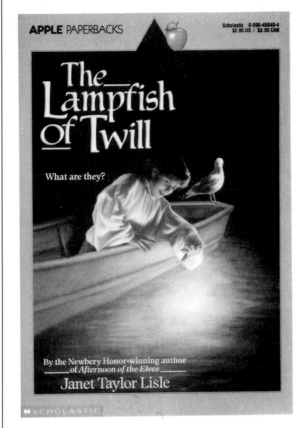

## SPOTLIGHT ON:
### THE LAMPFISH OF TWILL

In this exciting novel of fantasy, imagination, and adventure, orphaned Eric lives on the storm-washed coast of Twill with his aunt Opal. He befriends Ezekiel Cantrip, an old fisherman, who leads Eric down a whirlpool into an ancient and beautiful world in the center of the earth.

writer of the book, I must have special knowledge," she says. "I get many letters demanding to know whether the village is real, or made by Sara-Kate."

Some readers suspect Janet is deliberately keeping this information from them. "The truth is," says Janet, "I don't know any more than they do. That book has a sort of existence of its own. I was the one who wrote it and brought it into being and made the parts work, but

the mysteries at the center of the book are as perplexing to me, the writer, as they are to the reader."

## ANSWERING A TRICKY QUESTION

A shy boy at the back of a large school auditorium once asked Janet, "Have you ever seen an elf?" Janet answered that question carefully. She suspected the boy meant more than one thing. On the surface, he was wondering if she had seen an elf. But beyond that, "he was asking, I think, how much of my real self was involved in this book I had written, how much I was putting on for children. Was this something I made up because I was writing for children, or was I truly involved in the process?"

She answered, "I think perhaps I've seen bits and pieces of elves about in the world. I can't say that I've ever seen a whole elf, but I'm always on the lookout." This seemed to be the answer to the real question he was asking, which was about how much she believes in the importance of her writing.

## LISTENING FOR VOICE

To Janet, writing a new book is like meeting a new person. "That's why we read, too," she says "so we can have entirely different experiences." As a writer, Janet takes this one step further. "Writers have all these extraordinary tricks at the ends of their fingers, strings they can pull to make the illusion of life and story spring alive in the head, so why not use them?"

When she begins a new book, she tries hard to hear the book's "voice." For example, she began *The Lampfish of Twill* with the sound of the sea in her ear. The rolling sound of rushing waves played at the back of her imagination as she constructed characters and invented the plot.

"The next most important thing for me is to become acquainted with my characters," she says, "because they carry along the story."

Understanding her characters helps Janet make decisions as she writes. "There are many times when I come to a crossroad and can't decide whether to go here or there, how the plot should unfold." For Janet, the answer lies in understanding what a character would do. "You must follow that road in the direction it leads, knowing the character's personality in its million different details—clothing, beliefs, the sorts of food a person likes to eat, the way a person walks, his or her facial expressions, and ways of speaking to other people." At that point, Janet believes, "you can tell the story more effectively, because you can be absolutely true to the nature of that character."

> **"The next most important thing for me is to become acquainted with my characters because they carry along the story"**

Janet says the way she writes is similar to the way waves lap up at the shore. "At the beginning of every day, I go back and reread the story I am working on. I read up to where I left off

## A WRITING ACTIVITY
### from Janet Taylor Lisle

Lots of Janet's readers have written her to suggest other possible endings to *Afternoon of the Elves*. She likes this and suggests that you try to do the same thing. What do you think happened to Sara-Kate? What did Hillary do afterward? Try the same activity with other books you have read that seem to live on beyond their pages.

the day before, then I write on. The next day, I read back and push it forward again. Every time I go back over the territory that I've covered, I change it a little bit. The whole book grows and changes under my fingertips, right to the very end."

What does she hope her readers will take away from her books? "I would like to think that my books open up doors in the imagination, that they would entice a child to think in new ways." Not that Janet wants to enforce any special type of morality or behavior. "Many of the children in my books behave in ways that the adults truly wish they would not," she says.

Her hope for the influence she might have on her readers goes back to perception. She wants her readers to realize that "there are ways of looking at the world. Not just one way, but many ways. There are many frames to put around a truth." ∎

# Margaret Mahy

**BORN:** March 21, 1936, in Whakatane, New Zealand
**CURRENT HOME:** Lyttleton, New Zealand

**SELECTED TITLES**

**The Haunting**
1982

**The Boy Who Was Followed Home**
1983

**The Changeover: A Supernatural Romance**
1984

**Aliens in the Family**
1986

**The Tricksters**
1987

**The Great White Man-Eating Shark**
1990

**The Seven Chinese Brothers**
1990

**A Lion in the Meadow**
1992

**The Changeover**
1994

**The Pirate Uncle**
1994

Writer Margaret Mahy confesses jokingly, "When I'm ready to start a book, I think I hear a sort of voice telling me the story. My primary feeling about a book is the way it sounds." Sometimes, though, she also sees vivid pictures in her head. When she's reached that point, Margaret knows it is time to start writing, and she does. As she develops the plot, the other parts of her imagination—the parts that supply the funny scenes or the scary turns and twists that characterize her work—emerge.

When Margaret was a child, she wanted animals to like her. She drew on that memory to write *The Boy Who Was Followed Home* but exaggerated it, of course. She could have written about a boy who was followed home by guinea pigs. But she thought it would be funnier if he were followed home by a startling number of hippopotamuses. Her stories often have a basis in reality, but she admits, "I do change the events."

## WRITES QUICKLY, REVISES SLOWLY

It may take Margaret two weeks to write a short story, but revising can take much longer. She calls her process of revision "finding the pattern in a story." When she understands what a story is trying to say and how it should meander, she understands how to edit it. "Then I know where to trim pieces or add pieces, how to trim the middle area or stop the ending from being so drawn out," she says.

Finding the right pattern in a novel takes much longer, though by the time she starts writing a book she usually knows how she wants it to begin. "In some ways, I've talked that part through," the writer explains. "I know how it's going to end, more or less. But there are parts in the middle I'm not too sure about."

Some of her novels, such as *The Haunting* and *The Changeover*, actually began as short stories. "I wrote them and then put them aside until I had time to think about a longer book."

One of Margaret's easier tasks is to create characters. She usually has a clear idea of their interests, ideas, motivations, and of what goes on inside their heads. On occasion, though, a character has been harder for Margaret to get to know, such as the heroine in *Memory*.

"When I started writing the book, I had no idea of the way she was going to behave, or the relationship she'd have with the hero, Johnny.

For a long time, she was a mystery to me," Margaret admits. For that reason, the work went slowly. "When I began to write the book," says Margaret, "I had to change her. I had to adapt her in quite a lot of ways."

In the past, Margaret wrote her

stories in longhand, skipping every other line. When she went back to revise, she would write in different colors, "so the crowded words in the middle of the lines would be easier to read." She did it to entertain herself, too. "When the page became so untidy that I couldn't read the story, I'd type it for the first time," she says. "the minute I typed it out, I'd find there was a lot wrong with it. Then with clear print on the page, I'd start correcting it again. Though she now uses a computer, she still follows the same process of writing one day, revising the next.

Writing with a computer has changed Margaret's work in important ways. She sometimes feels as if she's lost something in the transition. When she worked in longhand, she'd often cross something out in such a way that she could still see it when she went back over it again. Sometimes, she'd decide she liked a passage the way it was in the first place and put it back. Now, when she corrects lines on a computer, says Margaret, "I wipe out the preceding words and replace them with others. I don't get the juxtaposition of one idea over another the way I did when a manuscript was corrected by hand." To hold on to that part of her process, she sometimes keyboards her original ideas on the word processor, then prints them and corrects her work by hand, as she did years ago.

## KEEPING IN TOUCH

Margaret begins each workday by answering letters from her readers. "I like to be in touch with kids," she says, and has often gone on long book tours, visiting children throughout her homeland, New Zealand, and in other countries, especially the United States. She enjoys communicating with her readers, finding kids' questions

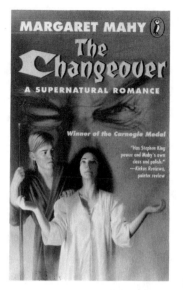

**MARGARET MAHY**
*The Changeover*
A SUPERNATURAL ROMANCE

Winner of the Carnegie Medal

"Has Stephen King power and Mahy's own class and polish."
—*Kirkus Reviews, pointer review*

## SPOTLIGHT ON:
### THE CHANGEOVER

When Laura's brother, Jocko, becomes very sick, Laura must decide whether or not she's willing to change into a supernatural being, with special powers able to help her brother. This story is exciting, strange, and unusual, and might just bring you to question what's real...and what isn't.

interesting to answer.

Once, in Ohio, she met a boy who asked, "Why do your stories always end well for the good people and badly for the bad people?" Margaret liked that question. "I told him, basically that most of the time, stories end up well for the good people because although stories are set up to entertain us, they are also expected to strengthen us. My stories are meant to be models for behavior." She adds, "Many folktales deal with the triumph of a good, kind, simple person rather than a rich, powerful, clever person. Folktales are one of the ways people make sense of their own lives."

One of the most challenging books Margaret has written is *The Tricksters*. "There were twelve characters that had to be acknowledged and developed," she says. "There were times when I wondered, 'What's gone wrong with this book?' I slowly realized that the problem was that I had to give so many characters something to say, some sort of position to hold." Recognizing that the task was a difficult one gave her the encouragement to tackle it again.

## ALWAYS A WRITER

Margaret started writing when she was seven years old. "My mother saved the first story I ever wrote," she says. "It was about a boy called Harry who was very lazy," Margaret remembers. "One day, Harry followed a golden pheasant to the house of a witch. The witch made him work for her. If he didn't, she'd beat him up with a broomstick. When he got over being lazy, she asked him to go home. When he woke up, it was a dream. It's got a good structure," she says, content that her first work showed a glimmer of promise. Margaret still has the story, and it interests her to look at it and to show it to children. "It was obviously based on other stories I'd read, and had to do with bad people being made good." As we know, this has been an important theme for Margaret all her life.

What advice does Margaret have for would-be writers? "I think it's very important to keep on writing. When I was small and at school, I knew only two other people who liked to write. Now, writing is part of the school program. I think the school programs now are producing better writers in many ways. The stories I wrote aren't any better than the ones today, but I kept on. My friends stopped writing in high school, but I continued. It's quite important to persist, in spite of disappointments."

> **"The ability to read and write gives you a bit more power in the world."**

Margaret still draws on her childhood memories for her stories. "I think that certain sorts of experiences I had in childhood remain with me quite strongly," she says. "They're a bit like information that comes in from space via satellites. Scientists receive a lot of information in code over a very short time. Then they spend a lot of time unraveling the code."

Not everybody should become a writer, of course. But Margaret says she feels sorry for people who don't like to write. "The ability to read and write gives you a bit more power in the world," she says. Conversation is the most important way to communicate, of course. But with writing, says Margaret, you have an advantage. "When you're writing, you can take your time and think about what you want to say. You can become more accurate about your thoughts." ∎

## A WRITING ACTIVITY
### *from Margaret Mahy*

Take an event that really happened to you and turn it into a fantasy. An example? "Once I drove my car off the road and into a ditch. People driving by stopped to see if they could help. The first four said it really wasn't possible. But the fifth person said, 'It's only a little car. Let's lift it up.' So we did.

"Feel free to change the tale, if you like. Perhaps a king drove off the road and got stuck in the ditch. Animals might help: a big blue buffalo, a snake on a skateboard—even a snake on a snakeboard." Won't that be fun!

# Gloria D. Miklowitz

**SELECTED TITLES**

**The Love Bombers**
1980

**Close to the Edge**
1983

**After the Bomb**
1985

**The War Between the Classes**
1986

**Love Story, Take Three**
1987

**Goodbye Tomorrow**
1987

**The Emerson High Vigilantes**
1989

**Suddenly Super Rich**
1989

**Anything to Win**
1989

**Standing Tall, Looking Good**
1992

**Desperate Pursuit**
1992

**The Killing Boy**
1993

**Boiling Point**
1994

**Past Forgiving**
1995

**BORN:** May 18, 1927, in New York, New York

**CURRENT HOME:** La Canada, California

Gloria D. Miklowitz is a very curious person. "I like to do a lot of research," she says. "In another lifetime, I might have been an investigative reporter." When she approaches a topic for one of her books, which are often about difficult, controversial subjects, Gloria plunges in, trying to collect direct experiences.

An example is her research for the book *The Love Bombers*, which is about religious cults. Against her family's wishes, Gloria spent a weekend on a retreat with a cult, the Moonies, followers of the Reverend Sun Myung Moon, to see how it felt being on the inside of such an organization. The cult leaders were very suspicious of her motives and avoided telling her anything negative about their lives. She told them, "When I leave, I'm going to find former [members of your cult] and hear their stories, so you might as well be honest with me now." The book she ended up writing presented both sides of cult life. She let her readers decide whether the cult lifestyle was healthy.

Says Gloria, "Many of the books I write leave the reader with no pat answer, but instead provide a rounded view of a problem and options to choose from." She has written about a number of problems in society, including teenage suicide, child abuse, nuclear war, injustice, and more.

## A TIRELESS RESEARCHER

A description of the way Gloria set about writing one of her most well-known books, *After the Bomb*, explains a lot about her thoroughness and determination as a writer. The book addresses nuclear armament from a "what if?" point of view. What if a nuclear bomb, deployed by accident, destroyed the city of Los Angeles? Gloria wrote the book because she hoped to awaken her readers to the dangers of a buildup of nuclear weapons.

*"Many of the books I write leave the reader with no pat answer, but instead provide a rounded view of a problem and options to choose from."*

She started her research by talking with a professor at the California Institute of Technology. "I told him I wanted to show readers how the thousands of nuclear bombs in the world could lead to the end of all life, and that even a single nuclear bomb exploding over one city would be disastrous. The professor said the most likely scenario would be an isolated accident. "How about if the accident occurred to Los Angeles?" she asked.

The professor offered to describe the fallout pattern to her, but Gloria wasn't

ready yet. "First I went to the library. I read that a one-megaton aerial burst would completely flatten a city up to three miles out. There would be less and less destruction beyond that," Gloria says. The suburb where she lives, La Canada, is about eleven miles from downtown Los Angeles. She decided to set her story in La Canada. "I assumed we would survive but we'd have many fires and other damage. Even with the state and federal government wanting to help Los Angeles and its nearby cities, communities would be on their own for

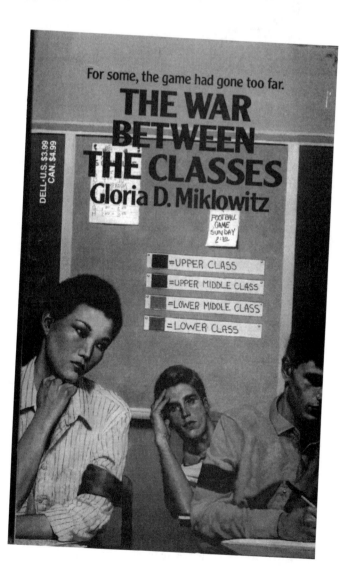

## SPOT LIGHT ON:
### *PAST FORGIVING*

At 15, Alexandra is thrilled to be dating Cliff, a popular, athletic senior with dark good looks. Cliff, however, tends to be very possessive. He's annoyed when she spends time with friends or talks to other boys—but she sees that as a sign of how much he loves her. Sometimes he gets angry and hits her, but she excuses him because maybe she provoked those feelings in him, and he is very apologetic afterward. Yet as Cliff's violence grows to extremes, even Alex comes to realize that there is a point at which no excuses are good enough, and no apologies can work.

at least the first forty-eight hours."

She wondered about contamination and radioactivity but decided that focusing on the effects of fallout might bog down the story. So she disposed of fallout by creating a Santa Ana wind condition that would blow contamination away from the city, out to sea.

Next, Gloria wanted to know how *her* community would respond to this disaster. She went to city hall in Los Angeles. Several floors underground she found civil defense headquarters, supposedly outfitted for any type of disaster. A lone man was on duty. "I asked him how he could conduct civil defense measures if his command center were buried beneath city hall." He did not have a believable answer and sent Gloria away with emergency-preparedness brochures that she says did not seem very useful.

Next, she went to the La Canada fire department. She asked the fire chief how he'd cope if downtown Los Angeles were destroyed and fires erupted in La Canada. The chief said. "Shock waves from the nuclear burst would probably destroy the firehouse. The roads would be clogged with overturned cars and downed power lines. We'd not be able to get our trucks out to fight fires and could only do what we could near the station." Water, too, would be a big problem because the source of the water supply would probably be disrupted.

To find out, Gloria went to the Department of Water and Power where she learned that wells in the hills supplied water to the nearby cities. "In the confusion of such a disaster, no one would think to turn off the valves controlling the water flow," she says. "Water would rush out of overturned hydrants until the wells ran dry. Without water, fires would rage unchecked."

The scenario was getting worse. Gloria visited the local hospital, about two miles from her home. She asked officials of the two hundred-bed hospital how they would treat a situation like this. "We only have enough power for forty-eight hours," said one official. "We couldn't expect much help before that time. The smoke would be too pervasive for any landing craft to come in. We'd be pretty much on our own."

With the recipe for a major disaster complete in her mind, Gloria got to work. She decided to feature her own two sons as the major characters in the book. Because she had always observed that her older son got more positive reinforcement than her younger son, she decided to make her younger son the hero in the book. "At fifteen, my older son was extremely verbal, mechanically inclined, decisive, and capable. Our younger son was quite the opposite, but he had many good traits we didn't give him credit for."

He is fiercely determined. "You could knock him down," she says, "but he'd get up and find a way to do whatever he set his mind to, regardless of the obstacles." Her younger son also has a wonderful sense of humor and is very good with people. She decided that these were exactly the traits a person needed to

> ## WORDS FROM THE AUTHOR:
>
> *"Each book is an adventure. Hard as it is to write, I get up and start writing, so I can find out what's going to happen."*

come out on top in the aftermath of a nuclear disaster.

Her thorough research and sharp characterizations paid off. The book that she wrote, *After the Bomb*, is compelling, terrifying, and quite convincing. She created a story that would go on to influence many readers.

## A WRITER'S SENSE OF SELF

A reader once asked Gloria, "Why do you keep on writing, when it's so hard?" She answered that her urge to write came from two sources: her sense of self as a writer and a need to say something of value to young people. "My sense of who I am is very much wrapped up in writing. It adds purpose, and structure to my days." She says that her writing urge is pushed by a spirit she calls a *dybbuk*. "It's a magical spirit that inhabits my brain. I have little control over it. The only way to cope with it is to write the stories." ■

## A WRITING ACTIVITY
### from Gloria Miklowitz

Take any book that you haven't read before. Read it halfway, or two-thirds of the way through, then come up with your own ending.

# Nicholasa Mohr

**BORN:** November 1, 1938, in New York, New York
**CURRENT HOME:** Brooklyn, New York

## SELECTED TITLES

**El Bronx Remembered: A Novella and Stories**
1975

**Felita**
1979

**Nilda: A Novel**
1986

**Going Home**
1986

**Uncle Nick's Gift**
1988

**In Nueva York**
1988

**Isabel's New Mom**
1993

**Growing Up Inside the Sanctuary of My Imagination**
1994

**Old Letivia and the Mountain of Sorrows**
1995

**Jaime and the Conch Shell**
1995

**The Song of El Coqui and Other Stories of Puerto Rico**
1995

"As a Puerto Rican child growing up in New York City, I felt invisible," says Nicholasa Mohr. "I never saw myself in books. I never read a book where there were any Puerto Rican children or Latinos. [It seemed as though] we were not significant, as though we never contributed to or affected the dominant society."

Because of this "invisibility," Nicholasa found it hard to imagine what life could be like outside her close-knit Puerto Rican New York City neighborhood. Nicholasa feels lucky to have grown up in a bilingual home. Her parents spoke Spanish primarily, and her six older brothers mainly spoke English. Though she is fluent in Spanish, she does not write in that language, since Spanish was not taught in schools. "Spanish is the language I turn to when dealing with my innermost emotions and feelings," she says.

Growing up in the Bronx, the girl was treated differently than her brothers. "They had more freedom," she observes. "I was watched all the time." Did she resent this? "Yes, I had to do many more chores around the house than they did." But the writer has used that experience to her benefit: Many of those feelings were expressed in *Nilda* and *El Bronx Remembered.*

Other small details of life in that place and time crop up in those books, too. For example, like the mother in *El Bronx Remembered*, Nicholasa's mom kept a chicken in the kitchen. But the Mohrs' chicken was not called "Joncrofo" Its name was "Cru Cru".

Nicholasa's childhood contained tragedy. Her father died when she was eight years old. Her mother was forced to work hard to support the family, which broke the woman's health. Despite the stress, Nicholasa's mother continued to encourage her daughter, praising her "God-given talents." She would often say to Nicholasa: "Someday you must study so that you can become an important artist, make an important contribution to the world, and really be somebody."

"These words of encouragement always made me feel better," remembers Nicholasa. "Painting and drawing were my first loves. They were the skills that set me apart from most of the other children in school. For example, I would volunteer to design and paint the sets for the class play. Often I could ingratiate myself with even the most bigoted and intolerant teacher."

Nicholasa's mother taught her to believe in herself. To this day she describes her mother as the person in her life she most admires. "I wanted nothing more than to please her," says Nicholasa.

## PORTRAIT OF A YOUNG ARTIST

Nicholasa studied fashion illustration in high school. After she graduated, she hungered for more art training. She enrolled at the Art Students League in New York and began her formal training.

While many of her classmates saved money to study art in Europe, Nicholasa chose instead to study in Mexico. There she was impressed with the works of the great muralists, such as Diego Rivera, José Clemente Orozco, and others. Seeing their work firsthand had a tremendous impact on her as an artist.

Nicholasa met and married her husband at this time in her life. They moved into to a "wonderful old wooden house" to raise a family. There she built a large studio. She made large, bold paintings that were filled with words—

EL BRONX Remembered

A novella and stories

Nicholasa Mohr

## SPOTLIGHT ON:
### NILDA

The story of a Puerto Rican girl emerging from a child to a teenager in New York City, *Nilda* creates a realistic portrait of growing up strong and confident in spite of the humiliation of poverty.

and, as she points out, this was long before graffiti was a standard sight on city streets. Her paintings attracted interest, and she enjoyed her career as an artist.

## ARTIST TURNS WRITER

Before long, she was contacted by the head of a publishing company, who collected her art. The executive was intrigued by the words she used in her paintings and suggested that she try writing a book about her life. At first, Nicholasa rejected the offer. She was a visual artist, after all, not a writer! Then she thought it over: There were so few books for children about growing up as a Puerto Rican in America.

> *"As a Puerto Rican child growing up in New York City, I felt invisible."*

The transition from artist to writer was more difficult than she expected. After all, writing is lonely work. "When I was painting, I could listen to music on the radio. Someone could come in and offer an immediate reaction to my work. There's a certain amount of gratification in that. People can relate to you, can share your work spontaneously. It's like sharing a piece of music."

Writing, on the other hand, is a solitary pursuit. "I could work all day on one paragraph or page," she says. "It's kind of lonely, isolating." Then, too, in spite of a natural talent, her first writing projects did not go as smoothly as she would have liked.

Her first project was a collection of short stories about her childhood. It was rejected by the executive who suggested it but was accepted by another publishing company. With a contract for *Nilda* in hand, she went to an artists' colony to write her first book.

Nicholasa spent a summer in a small cabin at the colony and succeeded in writing the first hundred pages of her book. With that good start, she was soon able to finish *Nilda*, and her writing career was underway.

## FEELING INCLUDED

Many of Nicholasa's books have been about adolescents. Why? Because that period in her own life was so filled with troubles, the author surmises. The biggest problem facing young people today, she says, is one of inclusion. "In our society, we have a tendancy to specialize and categorize," she says. "One is not simply a doctor, one is a heart doctor, a specialist, an endocrinologist. We have a tendancy to categorize kids, too. We don't accept teenagers into the great society at large, and give them a real place. This is even more the case with youngsters of color."

In the community in which Nicholasa grew up, youngsters were usually included in all activities. "Children were taken out everywhere and taught how to behave and how to relate." Today, on the other hand "we're always sending our young people off to do kid things or teenage things. We're not including them in decisions, letting them feel part of the dominant group. That is a big problem. If they were always included, perhaps they would know how to behave."

## CUENTOS, CUENTOS

Storytelling was very much a part of Nicholasa's childhood. "Cuentos, cuentos [stories, stories], lots of storytelling," she says. "When I was a little girl, stories

> ### WORDS FROM THE AUTHOR:
> *"You don't have to be a professional writer—just write. You don't have to be a professional artist—just draw. It's a way to express yourself personally."*

often gave us joy. An adult would tell us a story. Things might be bleak, we might face incredible despair, then suddenly, we were all happy. It was like magic."

Storytelling is still important to her today. "I really want to be a good storyteller," she says. "That's my primary goal. Everything else is gravy after that. I hope my readers come away with a sense that they have gotten involved in a good story—not just read it, but shared it, and gotten involved." Nicholasa says she writes with a purpose: "I want people to enjoy reading my work as much as I enjoy writing it." ∎

## A WRITING ACTIVITY
### from Nicholasa Mohr

Create a self-portrait. Write what you like best about yourself and what you would like to change. Reflect on yourself. If you prefer, draw your self-portrait. Use this activity as a way to understand how you see yourself. If you're working with a friend, write a portrait of him or her and have your friend do the same for you. Then share the results with each other.

# Michael Morpurgo

**BORN:** October 5, 1943, in St. Albans, England
**CURRENT HOME:** Devon, England

Twenty years ago, Michael Morpurgo, a gifted writer with a strong sense of duty, felt he was at a standstill in his career as a teacher. He wanted to have a greater impact on all his students, especially the ones with low self-esteem.

Michael and his wife Clare sought the advice of educational experts. They wanted to know if there was any way to change schools so that a greater percentage of children would go on to succeed in life. What might make a real difference, the experts suggested, would be to "introduce students to extraordinary people and extraordinary experiences, which change their perceptions of things, so that the world becomes a lovely place, a rich place, a place they want to belong to, where people are kind to them." Children who have that experience, Michael and Clare reasoned, might say to themselves: "Yes, I've got a place. This is my place. I like it."

## PUTTING THE IDEA TO THE TEST

The Morpurgos took action. They started a program called Farms for City Children on their farm in the English countryside. The program is still thriving, twenty years later. Every year, one thousand children leave their tough city neighborhoods, forty at a time, to live on the farm for a week. They work side by side with the Morpurgos and other farmers, participating in the farm activities. They milk cows, clean the cow yard, and care for a variety of farm animals.

Does the week on the farm have positive results? "It doesn't change everyone, of course," says Michael. "But what it does do is just shine a light for one or two children who

### SELECTED TITLES

**King of the Cloud Forests**
1988

**Why the Whales Came**
1990

**My Friend Walter**
1991

**Waiting for Anya**
1991

**Twist of Gold**
1993

**Sandman and the Turtles**
1994

desperately needed it." Some children show a reaction to the world around them almost for the first time. "Suddenly, they're interested in other things. It works. No question about it," says Michael. "What you don't know is the degree to which it works. But then, you never do with education."

When the week is over, Michael and Clare rarely hear from their visitors. "It tends to be an experience that's intense. It becomes part of their imaginary world after that," says Michael. "Paradise week, in a sense. But it's a hard week, in many ways. They do learn about sad things as well as happy things."

A recent group saw an animal born dead. "Well, that was awful," says Michael. "But it was probably the first dead creature they've touched. That's the beginning of coming to terms with mortality. The next day, they saw calves born. And overall, they got wind and rain and mud and lovely sunshine."

The Morpurgos have started a second farm, in Wales. A third is being formed in Vermont, in the United States, by a friend of theirs. The owner of that farm hopes to help children from New York City.

## A TWO-SIDED LIFE

With one-thousand visitors to his farm each year, how has Michael managed to write more than forty books? He goes off by himself to a quiet place and focuses.

Michael began writing during his teaching days. "Originally, I wrote stories for the children in my classes," he says. His first stories helped him see that story writing is also an important way to reach children. "I suppose one story struck a mark, and I could suddenly see mouths opening and eyes widening, and I

thought, 'actually, this is quite fun.'" Since then, writing has become an even bigger part of his life. "I tend to be very absorbed by what I'm doing. I finish a project, and then I feel empty and unused, and useless unless there's another idea washing around inside my head."

### WORDS FROM THE AUTHOR:

"I was encouraged by my parents [to write], but I was very keen on doing everything outdoors. Books didn't interest me at all until I was in college."

## LETTING A STORY DEVELOP

"When I have an idea for a story, I don't try to write it too soon," says Michael. "You can't do it like that. You need time for the thing to develop. I call it dreamtime." For Michael, this dreamy period can last for as little as two or three days or as long as twenty years. "There's no way you can force it. It's like an egg. It's going to crack open and hatch when it's good and ready. You must sit on your egg. You must let it incubate, hatch, then let it grow its beak and legs."

Michael writes his first drafts "very, very quickly, like I speak." He rewrites his stories four or five times. Then he reads them aloud into a tape recorder. He listens to the story and, by hearing it, recognizes the changes he wants to make. "You know when things are going on too long, when things are diverting, when language becomes a bit overflowery." His wife helps him edit too. "She knows when I'm being vainglorious," he says.

## POWERFUL OBJECTS SURROUND HIM

As he writes, Michael looks out his window at green fields. He can see the town of Dartmoor, several miles away. "It's lovely," he says. "That's the most disconcerting thing, because I spend a lot of time looking out, though I know I'd better get on with my work." On the bookcase behind him are his published books, which he finds "rather useful when I get miserable."

He keeps objects on his desk that are part of the stories he writes. For example, the plot of *A Twist of Gold*, about a family that emigrates from Ireland to America in the 1840s, centers around a lucky piece of gold that comes down through the family. As he wrote the book, Michael kept such a piece of gold on his desk. When he worked on *Waiting for Anya*, the story of World War II Jewish refugees being smuggled across the Spanish border from France, he kept a piece of bearskin beside him. A bear plays an important role in the book.

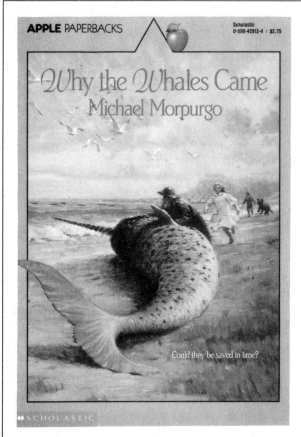

APPLE PAPERBACKS
Scholastic
0-590-42912-4 / $2.75

*Why the Whales Came*
Michael Morpurgo

Could they be saved in time?

SCHOLASTIC

## SPOTLIGHT ON:
### *WHY THE WHALES CAME*

This is a haunting mystery about a girl and boy who live on a lonely island off the coast of Great Britain. They befriend a strange old man known as the Birdman of Bryer. Together, they lift a curse from their island.

"I find it's very helpful to have something to touch while I'm writing," he says.

*"I'm stronger on place than I am on character. I have a very strong sense of where everything is happening. I must have that in order to be able to write."*

In *Why the Whales Came*, a remarkable fantasy set on the Isles of Scilly, *narwhals*, small whales with unicornlike tusks, are a key element in the story. As he wrote that book, Michael kept a narwhal's tusk nearby. "I found one in an antique shop. You can only get old ones now because it's forbidden for them to be sold," says Michael. "But they are extraordinary. When I first saw one, I thought it was a unicorn's horn. They're unbelievable."

Michael considers himself a visual writer. In fact, many of his books have been made into films. "I'm stronger on place than I am on character. I have a very strong sense of where everything is happening. I must have that in order to be able to write."

## TROUBLED TIMES

What is the biggest problem facing kids today? Michael says it's insecurity. "They don't know who they are," he says. "They're unsure of their surroundings and of the people around them. That lack of confidence is what breeds so much of the antisocial behavior today."

Michael grew up during the years of World War II and says that though that

## A WRITING ACTIVITY

*from Michael Morpurgo:*

Keep a diary, making careful notes on everyday things in your life. Simply jot down your thoughts. Be observant. For example, if you go to a zoo and see a giraffe, watch it move. Write about its height, its smell, what it eats and drinks. Think about what it must feel like to run your hand on its back. Include as many details as possible.

was a troubled time, it was simpler in many ways. "There were all sorts of terrible things going on, there always have been. But you weren't having to respond all the time to these immensely difficult things that children take on board very young today."

Michael feels that young people are so overwhelmed that "rules mean less and less. Authority seems to be weak uninteresting, and finally unloving." His work on the farm has shown Michael that "you can make relationships with children if you let them know very, very quickly just precisely where you're coming from and what you expect of them, and they'll respond."

Farms for City Children has provided a refuge for more than twenty thousand children. Michael's books have reached hundreds of thousands more, introducing readers to special places, notable characters, and important eras in history. Michael has found ways, after all, to reach the hearts, minds, and spirits of countless children. ■

# Katherine Paterson

**BORN:** October 31, 1932, in Qing Jiang, Jiangsu, China

**CURRENT HOME:** Barre, Vermont

## SELECTED TITLES

**The Great Gilly Hopkins**
1978

**Angels and Other Strangers**
1979

**Jacob Have I Loved**
1980

**Come Sing, Jimmy Jo**
1986

**Consider the Lilies**
1986

**Bridge to Terabithia**
1987

**The Sign of the Chrysanthemum**
1988

**Park's Quest**
1988

**The Mandarin Ducks**
1990

**Lyddie**
1991

**The King's Equal**
1992

**Flip-Flop Girl**
1994

"I try to explain to children," says Katherine Paterson, "that one idea does not a novel make. One idea is too thin. Those are the books that run out after a few pages." When Katherine is constructing a novel, she allows herself a considerable amount of time to let things she sees, thinks believes in, and feels strongly about mix together to form stories. Her novel *Park's Quest* is an example. "It's interesting," she says. "The various strands that make up the book have no relation to each other."

*Park's Quest* is about an eleven-year-old boy who goes to his grandfather's farm in Virginia to learn about his father, who died in the Vietnam War. While there, the boy makes some surprising discoveries.

The idea for the book began with a picture in Katherine's mind of an oriental-looking child in the hallway of the house where Katherine's father grew up. She wondered, "Who is she? What is she doing there?" She tried to write a short story based on that vision, but it didn't work. "So I dropped it into the file cabinet of my mind, the jumble bag, and forgot about it for a while."

Sometime later, a second important element in the story came to her. "We were in the home of close friends whose son had been killed in Vietnam," says Katherine. "They had just come back from the dedication of the Vietnam Memorial [in Washington, D.C.]. The effect of the service on them was powerful and healing. I realized that this monument was as important an image in our country as anything we have." Katherine went to see the monument, not because she hoped to write a book about it, but because of her relationship with her friends. As she expected, the monument had a deep effect on her.

Time passed, and other things influenced Katherine's imagination. Finally, the story was ready to be written. Although each individual element might not have made a powerful story by itself, somehow when they all came together in her imagination the story sprang to life. "These things happened over a period of years," says Katherine. "Suddenly, I realized that they belonged together."

## THE READER'S CHOICE

Many of Katherine's stories are about people who have to make tough decisions or who grapple with difficult problems as they are growing up. She doesn't believe that she writes these stories to help her readers grow or change in any particular way. "It's not the writer's business to make the reader 'become' something," she says. "It's the

> ## WORDS FROM THE AUTHOR:
>
> *"The time to start rewriting is when you can look at what you've written and say, 'Not bad.'"*

reader's choice. The reader can decide how to react, whether to be assaulted. The book is just going to sit there. If you can't stand the truth that the book has to give, then your mind doesn't have to accept it. That's one of the wonders of books. The reader gets what she's ready to get at the point that she's reading."

## MANY WAYS OF WORKING

Writing each book has been a different experience for Katherine. "Some are very

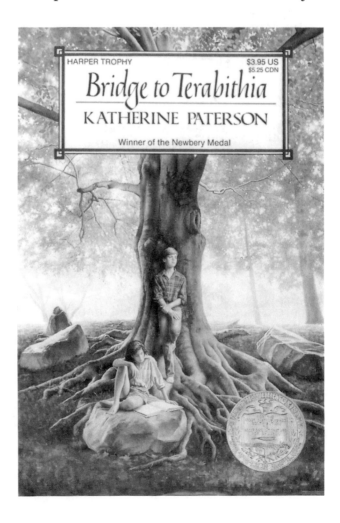

HARPER TROPHY $3.95 US $5.25 CDN
Bridge to Terabithia
KATHERINE PATERSON
Winner of the Newbery Medal

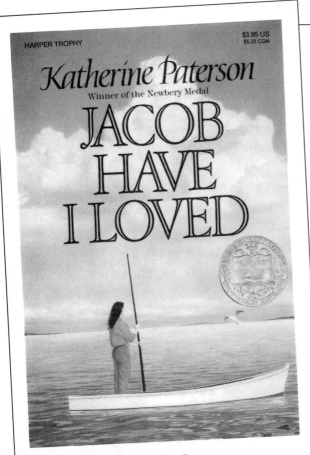

Katherine Paterson
Winner of the Newbery Medal

# JACOB HAVE I LOVED

## SPOTLIGHT ON :
### JACOB HAVE I LOVED

This is the story of the bitterness and jealousy a girl feels toward her twin sister. Sara Louise "Wheeze" Bradshaw is an ugly duckling who is sure she's unloved. Her delicate, capable twin sister gets all the attention. As the story unfolds, Wheeze comes to value her own gifts and abilities.

hard to start," she says. "Sometimes I play around on the typewriter for months, literally." If a book demands a lot of research, "I take mountains of notes, and then I lose about half of them. I'll have a vital scrap of paper, but I'll have no idea where it came from." When Katherine is really interested in what she's writing about, her ideas come faster and faster. "The more rapidly they come, the more rapidly they become unorganized."

Katherine writes on a computer, about which she has mixed emotions. "The computer has a quality the typewriter doesn't have," she says. "It seduces you into thinking you can be perfect. You spend today making yesterday's work perfect. Every time you go over it you can polish it a little bit."

> *"It's not the writer's business to make the reader 'become' something. It's the reader's choice."*

She first used a computer when she wrote *Come Sing, Jimmy Jo.* "With *Jimmy Jo*, I had four or five perfect first chapters, but nothing more. Then I moved it back to the typewriter, because there I can't make it perfect."

In Katherine's opinion, the whole purpose of a first draft is to get through the first draft. "I love to rewrite. The first draft is always messy and horrible." Then she puts it on the computer, "where I can rewrite to my heart's content. For editing and rewriting, computers can't be beat."

## A SYMPTOM OF SOMETHING ELSE

Like many writers, Katherine occasionally gets stuck. "Usually, like pain, it's a symptom of something else," she says. "I find that if I'm really stuck, I quit, go clean the kitchen, and go to bed. Very often, the first thing in the morning, the solution to the problem is there."

She got very stuck when she was writing *Park's Quest*. "I hit a stone wall. I had the book sketched out in my mind. I couldn't figure out how to get where I wanted to get." In this case, the problem didn't fix itself overnight. "I realized there was something drastically wrong with the first ten chapters. The plot was skewed. I hadn't gone at it in quite the right way." Once she rewrote the first ten chapters, there was no problem.

## "The first draft doesn't have to be good, it just has to be done."

She got stuck, too, when she was writing *The Bridge to Terabithia*. "When Leslie was going to die, I stopped. I didn't want her to die. I kept her alive by stopping."

Another way she deals with blocks is to sit down at her desk and say to herself, "Don't get up until you write two pages." She doesn't demand that the writing be of top quality. "I keep at that for a week or so. That usually breaks the dam."

## WROTE AS A CHILD

Katherine's childhood was quite unusual. She spent the first years of her life in China, where her father was a missionary. During World War II, she was evacuated with her family. They came to live in North Carolina, where Katherine's odd clothes and unusual British accent made her an outcast. As a result, she became an avid reader with a very vivid fantasy life.

Katherine wrote a lot as a child, but she remembers that nobody took her writing very seriously. "Most of it was an imitation of something else," she says, "what I thought I *ought* to be doing. I wrote a lot of imitations of Elsie Dinsmore (a children's writer who wrote sentimental books and was popular when Katherine was a child) and poems that sounded like basal readers."

Kids often ask her how she feels when she's writing about things that are sad or frightening. Katherine answers, "It rips me up. If something terrible happens to my characters, I'm in agony."

When people ask her what qualifies her to be a writer for children, Katherine answers: "I was once a weird little kid. I'm sure there are plenty of fine writers who have overcome the disadvantages of a normal childhood. It's just that we weird little kids do seem to have a head start." ■

## A WRITING ACTIVITY
### from Katherine Paterson

Somebody once sent me Agnes Stokes' diary. [Agnes Stokes is the scrawny little girl who attaches herself to Gilly in Katherine's book *The Great Gilly Hopkins*.] The diary tells the story from her point of view. I loved it. The kid did a wonderful job. It was Agnes looking at Gilly, rather than Gilly looking at Agnes. Try that yourself. Try to write a story from an unlikable character's point of view.

# Richard Peck

**BORN:** April 5, 1934, in Decatur, Illinois
**CURRENT HOME:** New York, New York

## SELECTED TITLES

**The Dreadful Future of Blossom Culp**
1983

**Remembering the Good Times**
1986

**Princess Ashley**
1988

**Secrets of the Shopping Mall**
1989

**Those Summer Girls I Never Met**
1989

**Through a Brief Darkness**
1989

**Dreamland Lake**
1990

**Unfinished Portrait of Jessica**
1991

**Don't Look and It Won't Hurt**
1992

**Blossom Culp and the Sleep of Death**
1994

Richard Peck visits one hundred classes each year. He's asked many questions. One question he is often asked is: "Do you live around here?" Richard thinks of this as the most encouraging question because it suggests that students think of him as a neighbor. "That's the best book review in the world. If I have sparked that kind of response, I've found a link between my readers and the characters. That's a good day. That keeps me writing."

Sometimes readers identify so closely with characters Richard has invented, they practically think he has written about them. "When readers identify with my characters," he says, "they identify on outrageously personal terms." Many readers connect with the character Blossom Culp, who appears in four of Richard's novels. "She's my most popular character," he says. "I find it very rattling, because I've heaped her with disadvantages. She's unattractive, she has a poor mother, no father, nothing, except wonderful spunk." Richard gets letters from girls who say: "I am Blossom Culp. Here is my picture."

Readers of Richard's books sometimes find themselves in situations parallel to those he describes, and they write to tell him so. Sometimes this makes him sad, especially when he gets letters about *Remembering the Good Times*, which is about teenage suicide. "A girl wrote me once and said she wished she had read it sooner," says Richard. He wished she had, too. "I didn't want to have to write that book," he says. "I didn't want to have to do that research. But I get the best letters from it." He believes it's his best book because his readers tell him so. "I wanted to dramatize the classic warning signs of teenage suicide in a responsible way that didn't oversimplify the situation," he says. "That was the lesson plan I set forth." (Richard is a former teacher.) "It was certainly worth doing."

He's glad to learn that the book is being taught in schools. "It needs teaching," he says. "Any novel without a pat, happy ending needs teaching." He says he gets a lot of letters from young people who loved the book but hated the ending. "So did I," says Richard. "The boy shouldn't have killed himself. He should have threatened to kill himself but not gone through with it." But to tell the story with that ending would be a departure from actual statistics. "The fact is, girls threaten to kill themselves three times more often than they actually do it," he says. "Three times as many boys kill themselves as girls. Girls use a threat of suicide as a plea for help. The boys are usually way beyond help."

As Richard wrote *Remembering the Good Times*, he was filled with foreboding. "I wrote it in grief," he says. "Every time I created something more about the character, I knew I was creating a human sacrifice." Since Richard was so unhappy writing the book, he wrote it as quickly as possible. And he's glad he wrote it, because he thinks it has opened up a lot of good discussion among teenagers about suicide. Maybe it's even saved some lives.

## TROUBLED TIME

Another difficult topic he's glad he's written about is divorce. "Adults tend to see divorce as a solution to a difficult situation," says Richard. "To young people, the divorce itself is the problem. Kids never wish their parents would get a divorce."

For this reason, he wrote *Unfinished Portrait of Jessica*. "I kept getting letters

## WORDS FROM THE AUTHOR:

*"I know I'm not gong to write as simple a story as my readers want, and as pat. They want the happy ending you don't have to earn. They can get it in their lives from their parents and teachers. They can't get it from me."*

Drew's on a cruise he'll never forget.

**RICHARD PECK**
Those Summer Girls I Never Met

DELL · 20457 · *U.S. $3.50 CAN. $4.50

## SPOTLIGHT ON:
### THOSE SUMMER GIRLS I NEVER MET

From Richard Peck's cruise-ship experiences, he wrote *Those Summer Girls I Never Met*, about Drew and Steph, ages almost sixteen and fourteen, who reluctantly take a Blatic cruise with their unusual grandmother, a retired singing star from the 1940s.

from girls saying, 'My father left, but of course, who wouldn't leave my mother.' As far as the girls are concerned," says Richard, "it's always the mother's fault." He hopes that this book helps children of divorce see the situation a little differently.

Richard also likes poking fun at the consumerism of teenagers. "That's why I wrote *Secrets of the Shopping Mall*," he

says. "I don't think it did any good but I decided it would be good to be on record. Nobody has ever challenged kids' crassness, and asked them what they're really trying to buy."

Common among all of these books, and among all the books Richard writes, is the use of theme as a starting point. "I go shopping for a theme and then start auditioning for characters. I can't tell these stories myself. I have the wrong vocabulary, the wrong memories."

*"Mark Twain got me started as a writer. I was looking high and low for proof that you could be a writer from the Middle West. There he was."*

He writes each book six times. Then he throws out the first chapter and rewrites it. In his opinion, the first chapter should be "the last chapter in disguise." In the first chapter he introduces his characters, his themes, and often a foreshadowing of the message he hopes to bring across. "It took me a while to figure this method out," he says. "For years, I would put elements in the first chapter, and then try to play them out later. There would be no way to do it. It was like trying to find a place to stand while building up a pile of earth. Now I write the book and then put the elements I need in the first chapter."

Richard writes in only one spot at his desk, positioned to look out over the Manhattan skyline. "I've finally come grudgingly to the electric typewriter," he says. "I can only write here, at my desk, not in airplanes, not in hotel rooms. I need places where I don't have to write."

To get himself started, and to help himself when he gets stuck, Richard polishes his collection of English brass. "Before I can write, the brass must be polished," he says, "so that I don't have to start work." In needing this type of outlet for his energies, Richard paraphrases a statement by E. B. White: "No writer can be expected to write a line until all the pictures in the world have been straightened."

## ADMIRES MARK TWAIN

All his life, Richard has admired the writer Mark Twain. Maybe that has something to do with his midwestern roots. He grew up in the small town of Decatur, Illinois. "Mark Twain got me started as a writer," says Richard. "I was looking high and low for proof that you could be a writer from the Middle West. There he was. Of course, he was just a little too big." But the fact that Mark Twain had come before him, with a similar background, gave Richard hope. "Blossom Culp is a female Huckleberry Finn," he says. "My father lived a Mark Twain boyhood and often told us nostalgic stories about it. To make Blossom Culp, I blended my father's memories with the character of Huckleberry Finn."

Richard did not become a writer immediately after college and the army; first he taught—for about fifteen years. The insights he gained into people and situations from this experience served as wonderful preparation for becoming a writer, he believes. One day, May 24, 1968, he walked out of a classroom as a teacher for the last time. The next day he began his career as a writer, giving himself the summer to see if he had what it takes.

Talent and luck prevailed. Richard hand carried his first finished manuscript to an editor one afternoon during the following September. The next morning, the editor called. "Start your second novel," he said. Richard hasn't stopped since.

When he's not writing, Richard has a second job: as a lecturer on cruise ships. "Two winters ago, I went around the world," he says. "This past winter, I went through the Panama Canal." On the ship, he also gives a course for grandparents about their teenage grandchildren. "They turn out in force," he says. "They are much more honest than parents. They are very concerned about their grandchildren." Richard always includes at least one elderly person in each of his novels, and he says that these cruises are his chance to be with older adults. ■

## A WRITING ACTIVITY
### from Richard Peck

Write about something that happened to you that would fit into a novel. When you choose the subject, think about experiences you've had that have changed you in some way, times when you were especially frightened, especially angry, especially aware of being alive.

# Robert Newton Peck

**BORN:** February 17, 1928, in Vermont
**CURRENT HOME:** Longwood, Florida

## SELECTED TITLES

**Path of Hunters: Animal Struggle in a Meadow**
1973

**A Day No Pigs Would Die**
1979

**Basket Case**
1979

**Soup**
1979

**Bango**
1982

**Hallapoosa**
1988

**The Horse Hunters**
1988

**Arly**
1989

**Arly's Run**
1991

**Soup's Hoop**
1992

**Soup Ahoy**
1994

**A Part of the Sky**
1994

Robert Newton Peck's childhood on a Vermont farm left an indelible impression on him. "My father was a Shaker," he says (Shakers were a religious sect of people in American history who believed in a simple, communal life of hard work.) "My mother probably was, too, to a lesser degree.

"There were an awful lot of Plain People around us," says Peck. He identifies with the scenes in *Witness*, a movie set among the Amish, another pacifist religious sect. "When they were raising that giant barn, that was my boyhood. I remember people who looked like that," he says, referring to the men and women in traditional clothes working as a team to build a barn for a neighbor.

Peck's childhood home was situated on a small dirt road outside a small town. "We were the sons and daughters of illiterate farmworkers, mill workers, and lumberjacks," says Rob. "Some of the folks in town called us uproaders. And we called *them* downhillers." There was friction between the two groups.

True to their pacifist beliefs, Rob's parents taught him never to fight. "I was never spanked," he says. "I never hit anybody. I was taught never to do that, that it was wrong." Instead, his family practiced turning the other cheek.

Though his family lived simply off the land, Rob remembers them as sophisticated "as regards animals and plants and trees." In Rob's opinion, "if you don't know nature, you're not sophisticated at all." He's unhappy that too many kids today think that hamburger starts out at a fast-food restaurant. He asks: "When was the last time you touched a cow?"

Rob has always remembered his father's advice: "Learn what's so. This will guide you through all your life."

These simple words are on Rob's mind quite a bit. "My father taught me what morality was," he says. "People don't know morality can be defined by three words: How Life Behaves. It isn't how you or I want it to behave, it's how life *actually* behaves."

He laughs when he gets holiday cards with drawings of the lion lying down with the lamb. "This doesn't take place in the real world, not in God's world," he says. "In nature, animals attack other animals." He likes thinking about how perfectly nature constructs itself. "When rabbits give birth to their babies, they are born blind and deaf, because that way they're totally insulated from the big attacking things of the world. They don't hear the owl hooting or the panting of the fox. If they did, they would move and die. They are tranquil. This keeps them alive."

> **WORDS FROM THE AUTHOR:**
>
> *"Complainers and gripers rarely amount to much. They're usually too occupied with wailing about people who are busily handling the chores."*

## A PROLIFIC WRITER

The author of more than sixty books, Rob laughs and says, "I don't write quality, I write quantity." He wrote one of his most well known books, *A Day No Pigs Would Die*, in just two and a half weeks. The same was true of the sequel, *A Part of the Sky*.

"With *Pigs*, my memory's chain got pulled. All of a sudden, the lanyard on the cannon yanked, and the pizza

splattered all over the wall!" Why was he able to write them so quickly? "Writing is very easy, if you write about what you know," he says.

While writing *A Day No Pigs Would Die*, he had "ten different titles." One day, while working on the last chapter of the book, he looked down and saw the sentence that later became the book's

## SPOTLIGHT ON:
## A DAY *NO PIGS WOULD DIE*

A Shaker boy growing up on a Vermont farm grieves when his pet pig is killed but also learns to be the head of the family when his father dies.

title. "It doesn't even have a correct noun and verb!" laughs Rob. Why did he use it, then? "At my father's funeral, all the men he killed pigs with were gathered there, all these poorly dressed people in wagons, and they kept coming and coming. The title just seemed so fitting."

Rob still remembers his father saying, six months before the older man died, "This is my last winter, Rob. I'm going to die. You've got to take care of your mother and your aunt. There isn't anybody else." When the time came, Rob was able to shoulder his responsibilities.

## THE WRITING LIFE

Rob has written in many different places. He has lived in many different places, too, because, he says, "it's tough to hit a moving target!" Once, he wrote from atop a big cypress tree. "I was scared to death," he remembers. "I was higher up than I had planned. That was more or less what I was firing for."

> *"Writing is very easy, if you write about what you know."*

When he gets ready to write, Rob buys a stack of yellow legal pads and a box of black felt-tipped pens. He laughs at friends and neighbors who rely on expensive electronic apparatus. "One guy I know, he's probably got ten rooms of equipment in his writing room," says Rob. "He couldn't write a grocery list. He couldn't write a letter to his mother."

## LOOKING BACK

Rob often talks about his school days, especially the first six years, which were spent in a "tumble-down, one-room, dirt-road school in rural Vermont." When he thinks about that school, he thinks about his teacher, Miss Kelly. "She believed in scholarship, manners, and soap," he has written. "But more, she believed in me. In all of us, telling us that in America you don't have to be what you're born."

The youngest of seven children, Rob was the only member of his family to go to school at all. His parents didn't even want *him* to go to school. "When I finally introduced Papa to Miss Kelly, initially he said nothing," wrote Rob. "But he took off his hat."

Miss Kelly recognized the importance of this small gesture. "Thank you," she said, "for giving me Robert. I shall try to be deserving of your trust."

His father nodded and said to Miss Kelly, "Well, whatever he breaks, I'll pay for."

Rob kept up contact with Miss Kelly

throughout her long life. He dedicated many books to her and credits her with helping him achieve his full potential. "I am most thankful that she lived to share in my success as a writer," he says. ∎

# A WRITING ACTIVITY
### *from Robert Newton Peck*

Write about something tangible. Don't start out trying to write about the big things, like love and death. Rummage around your house and find an object that interests you. Jot down its color, its shape, its texture, its size, its smell (if any), its features, its uses, and its potential uses. Describe the object in as many ways as you can.

# William Sleator

**BORN:** February 13, 1945, in Havre de Grace, Maryland
**CURRENT HOME:** Boston, Massachusetts

W hen William Sleator is going to write a book, one of his first steps is to brainstorm. "I'll get an idea, and if it requires research, I'll do research," he says.

In this brainstorm mode he writes between forty and one hundred pages. By the end of that time, he often has an effective plot and characters. William doesn't write from an outline but from a general sense of what he wants to say. "Whatever my idea was when I began to write, I diverge from it when I get into the book," he says. By the time he gets to the end of the first draft, says William, "I know what I'm doing. Then I fix the beginning of the book to lead into the ending."

Often, William begins with an idea or a theory from the world of science that he finds interesting. Then he devises characters that have reasons to be involved with that theory. For example, in *Strange Attractors*, William wrote about an alternate reality, called Chaos, a world where everything is just a little bit "off." Before he started writing the book, he read about scientific theories of chaos.

Then he devised his characters by asking himself, "What type of person would be likely to get involved with this?" He came up with "good guys," who would do anything in their power to keep the world from slipping into Chaos. And he devised "evil twins" to the "good guys," who had an interest

## SELECTED TITLES

**Into the Dream**
1979

**Singularity**
1985

**Interstellar Pig**
1986

**The Boy Who Reversed Himself**
1986

**The Duplicate**
1988

**Fingers**
1990

**Strange Attractors**
1990

**Among the Dolls**
1991

**House of Stairs**
1991

**The Spirit House**
1991

**Oddballs**
1993

**Different Dimensions**
1994

in making Chaos come to pass.

To amuse himself, William decided to make the evil characters a little more appealing than the good characters. He also made fun of some trends in society. In this book, the good guys eat health food but are fairly unhealthy and unappealing in general. "I thought it would be funny to make fun of health food," says William. The bad guys have hundreds of vices, but they're more interesting and attractive.

**WORDS FROM THE AUTHOR:**

*"My advice to kids who like to write is this: Remember, it's never good enough the first time. You have to revise. Lots of times."*

Though he claims not to believe in outside inspiration, he reasons, "If I had such a thing as a muse, then I would say that these masks are my muses." He has a few favorites among the masks. "The weirdest are from Bali. A couple of the ones from Bali are cyclopses, with one eye in the middle of the forehead. Those sort of . . . inspire me."

When writing during the day, William uses a computer. At the end of the day, he prints out his work and goes over

## THE WRITER'S INTERESTS

The subject of time is also very important to William and figures in many of his books. "Not just time travel, but also the anomalies of time," he says. "In my book *Singularitiy*, there are twins who find a place where time goes faster. I love the idea—which happens to be a fact—that gravity slows down time. Acceleration also slows down time. These ideas are so fantastic in that they're completely real."

Another subject that interests him is extrasensory perception. "It's one of my interests, even though I don't believe in it," he says. "I believe in science. All the scientific experiments that have been done show that people cannot communicate by thinking."

## THE WRITER AT WORK

William works at a big desk in a small study. He is surrounded by a number of grotesque masks from all over the world.

what he's written. He scratches things out and makes changes. The next day, he looks at those changes and decides whether or not to incorporate them into the text. "Every day I start out working over what I wrote the previous day," he says. "That gets me going and builds up my momentum so I can start writing again."

Some authors feel as if their characters "tell them stories," that the characters themselves take on lives and create dialogue of their own. That is not the case for William. "I don't think anything has been given to me at all," he says. "It's all hard work, that's what it is. You just sit down and sweat."

## SOUTHEAST ASIAN INSPIRATION

William loves to travel, particularly in Southeast Asia. He especially enjoys spending time in small villages along the border of Cambodia and Thailand. William has traveled there regularly since 1986. He stays in Southeast Asia for as long as he can, typically about two

or three months, which is the longest visa he can get. Though recently he's been writing a book set in Thailand, at first he spent time there writing about his childhood. Perhaps it was the distance in space and time from his experience that gave him the clarity he needed. "It was interesting," he says. "Being immersed in this foreign culture made it possible to write about my past, because it gave me insight into growing up in the Midwest. The book became *Oddballs*.

## A MUSICIAN TURNED WRITER

Growing up, William wasn't sure whether he wanted to be a writer or a musician. He studied musical composition for many years and worked as a ballet accompanist as well. He also composed music.

How does writing music compare to writing books? He doesn't think the two processes are alike at all. "Usually, music doesn't really mean anything. It's just sound." Writing a book, to William, is much more like "solving a puzzle. You have to make everything fit together."

"I never revised the music I composed very much," he says. "I would just sit down and write. I know composers who do revise, but I never felt that it was part of the process."

## PROBLEMS KIDS FACE TODAY

William thinks a lot about how difficult it is for kids to grow up today. He's particularly concerned about problems caused by peer pressure. "I think fitting in with other kids is very strongly on their minds," he says. "I wish they didn't

## A WRITING ACTIVITY
### from William Sleator:

Keep a journal. In it, write down things that happen to you. You can write about special events, feelings, and ideas; or write plans, wishes, or dreams. At a later time, reread what you wrote. It will be a great source of ideas.

care so much about that."

William came from a background where individuality was strongly emphasized. "Not that I didn't care what everyone thought about me—of course I did. But at the same time, we were trained to appreciate our own uniqueness and not to try to be like everybody else."

> *"Every day I start out working over what I wrote the previous day. That gets me going and builds up my momentum so I can start writing again."*

That's a message William likes to bring across in his books. "So what if some kids are a bit different. They're going to grow up anyway, and they will be better off for being independent."

William enjoys reading and always has. When asked to name a favorite author, he mentions Muriel Spark, author of *The Prime of Miss Jean Brodie*. "She writes with economy," he says. "She can communicate vast amounts of information in few words." That's how William tries to write. "I think I'm too wordy, even so." Because he likes controlling his own wordiness, William likes writing for young adults. "I'm writing for a lot of kids who are not necessarily big readers. So I can't write very long books." ■

**WILLIAM SLEATOR**

**SINGULARITY**

Through a door into another world they touched the awesome power of time

## SPOTLIGHT ON:
### *SINGULARITY*

"The book of mine that I think has the most unusual ideas is *Singularity*. Lots of people have written books about time travel. There aren't many books about a place where time goes faster. The funny thing about it is that after I wrote the book, I participated in a conference about Robinson Crusoe. I found out that in a lot of ways that character dealt with being stranded alone for a long period of time and those strategies were the same my children used when they had to stay within a six-by-twelve foot building for a year."

# Todd Strasser

**BORN:** May 5, 1950, in New York, New York
**CURRENT HOME:** Larchmont, New York

## SELECTED TITLES

**Angel Dust Blues**
1981

**Friends Till the End**
1981

**Workin' for Peanuts**
1983

**Turn It Up!**
1985

**Wildlife**
1987

**The Accident**
1990

**Beyond the Reef**
1991

**The Diving Bell**
1992

**Free Willy**
1993

**Help! I'm Trapped in the First Day of School**
1994

**How I Changed My Life**
1995

For Todd Strasser, writing for teenagers satisfies the author's need to explore feelings about events in his past. Whether it's *Angel Dust Blues*, a book about a boy in trouble with drugs, or *Friends Till the End*, which deals with losing a friend to cancer, creating stories lets the author think about some events in his youth. "A lot of those things really happened, if not to me, then to people I was very close to," says Todd. "I had friends who were involved with drug sales, with taking drugs, and overdosing on drugs. I did lose a friend to cancer. Writing those books was a way of dealing with those incidents. In a sense, the first two books were written for me."

Once his first two books were published, Todd was happy to discover he was able to reach readers far and wide. "I've gotten mail from kids incarcerated in Alaska and Ohio. They wrote their reactions to *Angel Dust Blues*," says Todd. "It seemed to make a real impression on them. And I've gotten a few letters from kids who have friends with cancer, as in *Friends Till the End*."

This encouraging response convinced him that fiction could touch teenagers with important messages about life. With that in mind, he went on to write about relationships

(*Workin' for Peanuts, A Very Touchy Subject*), self-esteem (*Complete Computer Popularity Contest* and *How I Changed My Life*), peer pressure (*The Accident*), even playing in a rock and roll band (*Rock n' Roll Nights, Turn It Up!, Wildlife*).

His books have required little research. (An exception is *Beyond the Reef*, an adventure story about diving for treasure in ancient shipwrecks.) Usually, when he's in the middle of a book, he's highly attuned to his subject. Day or night, he reads and listens for tidbits, articles, or television or radio stories that relate to the story. "So in my conversations with people, whatever comes up that seems appropriate, I soak up and use."

These days, he's writing a novel about the universe of electronic communication, known as cyberspace. "I've been working on it for a long time," says Todd. "I've collected all kinds of information about the so-called electronic superhighway."

APPLE PAPERBACKS

**HELP!**
I'M TRAPPED IN THE FIRST DAY OF SCHOOL
...forever!

Todd Strasser

SCHOLASTIC

## WORDS FROM THE AUTHOR:

*"Trying to write a story without knowing the end is like trying to make a road without knowing where it's going to go. You can't do it."*

## THE PROCESS

Creating on a computer, Todd finds that he rewrites extensively. "By the time I get to the end of the book, I've rewritten the beginning many times."

The author outlines every book he writes, thinking the story through ahead of time. But he doesn't always stick to the outline. "No matter how well I outline my books, there are always things that have to be changed," he says. "Once the characters come to life, things don't always work out as I initially imagined."

He's especially concerned with foreshadowing—scattering hints or clues through a story to indicate a later event. Todd provides an imaginary example: "If, on page eighty, Jeremy asks Walter for help, the reason for Jeremy's request must trace back to an event at the beginning of the book." Todd is especially aware of this because he's an observant reader of other authors' works. "I hate when things come out of the blue," says Todd. "Like suddenly on page one hundred and twenty the kid becomes an expert skier."

Outlining a book in advance also keeps Todd from getting writer's block. "If I get stuck, then I know I've got a major problem on my hands. I have to go back and reconsider the whole structure of the story."

## A PEEK INSIDE

Todd writes in a sunny room on the third floor of his home. "I have three windows with southern exposure," he says. "From those windows I see lots of trees and my neighbor's house." From another set of windows he sees a little park. In winter, with the leaves off the trees, he can spot Long Island Sound. Some days he gets up early and goes up to his workroom, where he watches the sun rise. "I like to observe life going on around me," says Todd. "Most of that life is nature—raccoons and squirrels and birds."

The author writes all year long but is most productive during the "inside months" of autumn, winter, and early spring. "By the time May or June rolls around, I'm eager to get out of the house."

The author's workroom is decorated with posters of game fish. "Fishing is something I enjoy immensely," says Todd, who shares a boat with a friend.

When he's writing, Todd feels he's gone somewhere "else"—into the world of his imagination. "When I'm really involved in writing and I suddenly go outside, the transition feels awkward," he says. His mind is still on what he was just doing. "This used to be much more dangerous when I lived in New York City. On at least two occasions I found myself standing in the middle of busy West End Avenue: I hadn't even looked at the light, and there was traffic

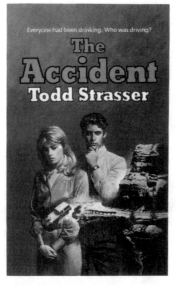

Everyone had been drinking. Who was driving?

## The Accident
### Todd Strasser

## SPOTLIGHT ON:
### *THE ACCIDENT*

After four of his friends leave a beer party and suffer a fatal accident, eighteen-year-old Matt senses something strange about the police investigation. He suspects a cover-up to hide the identity of the pereson really responsible for the accident. Matt takes a risk to bring forth the truth.

barreling all around me."

Distractions rarely bother Todd when he's working. "I can write under fairly demanding circumstances," says Todd. "I've been in rooms writing while people were sanding floors and doing major construction in the next room. Because of my schedule, I even write in airports and on airplanes."

The speed with which Todd writes depends entirely on the book. "Some books come much more easily than others. There is no relationship to a book's quality or popularity and the speed with which I write it. I've worked for years on books that everybody hated. I've worked just a few weeks on books that people adore."

As he writes, Todd hears his characters speaking. "I try to use words to create a picture that the readers can recreate in their own heads," he says.

Todd admits that his writing is "a little spare on description. I don't think about it that much. To me, dialogue and characterization are more important. I try to do a lot with dialogue."

He begins each new book with "a big burst of energy. "The first few weeks, I'm really producing a lot of pages. When I get to the middle, I slow down and writing becomes a struggle. As I get to the end, I speed up again."

When asked what he thinks the biggest problem is facing young people today, Todd answers: "Choices. Freedom. Some kids just can't handle it." He doesn't think kids are to blame for this situation. "It's just that there's too much out there for them to pick and choose from. There are too many traps and pitfalls. I feel bad for kids today. Their lives are too complicated and busy."

> *"By the time I get to the end of the book, I've rewritten the beginning many times."*

The solution? "Well, for a start, it would really help if all the guns in the world were banned," he says. Though, he admits, "I'm not always pragmatic about these things."

Todd remembers having a stable childhood in a middle-class area of Long Island, New York. "I played a lot of sports on the streets." Todd's grandfather was a big influence. "He lived near the water. He had a boat and liked to take everybody fishing." That may be where Todd got his love of the water. Todd's writing ability may have come from this grandfather as well. Todd reacalls, "He liked to make up funny poems and songs."

Todd's grandfather owned a movie house in New York City. "I had some minor exposure to the movie business when I was growing up," says Todd. "That may have something to do with why I write novelizations." Novelizations are books based on movie scripts. Todd has written many best-selling novelizations, including *Home Alone*, *Honey I Blew Up the Kids*, and *Free Willy*.

"When your family owns the movie house but is not making movies themselves, you're still, to some extent, in the movie business. You're part of the excitement. You get to see what's coming up." As a novelizer, Todd tries to recreate that good feeling he remembers from the script. He loves working on novelizations. "I feel I have a connection to something exciting."

What advice does Todd offer to aspiring writers? Learn to be a good reader. "The process of rewriting is really looking at your work and saying to yourself: 'Is this good enough?' If you haven't formed some sense of what is good enough, you don't know the answer." ∎

## A WRITING ACTIVITY
### from Todd Strasser

In five sentences, describe how you behave and feel on a very hot day. First, think about some things you might see, some things you hear, some things you smell. Jot them down. Then weave the sensory words into a picture, but avoid *hot*, *heat*, *boiling*, and *broiling*. Now describe a cold day. This time, avoid the words *cold*, *frigid*, or *freezing*.

# Joyce Carol Thomas

**BORN:** May 25, 1938, in Ponca City, Oklahoma
**HOME:** Caryville, Tennessee

J oyce Carol Thomas lives without a lot of fear. And she loves to talk to people about writing—especially to groups of students. So when she was asked to visit a group of students in California who had been fighting with each other, she refused to be afraid, although the situation was tense.

## SELECTED TITLES

**Marked by Fire**
1982

**Bright Shadow**
1983

**The Golden Pasture**
1986

**Water Girl**
1986

**Journey**
1988

**A Gathering of Flowers: Stories about Being Young in America**
(Editor)
1990

**When the Nightingale Sings**
1992

**Brown Honey and Broomwheat Tea**
1993

The school that asked her to speak had mostly white students (Joyce herself is African-American). Another school nearby had mostly African-American students. Fights had been breaking out between students at the two schools, and Joyce was asked to speak to an assembly of students from both schools. She was concerned about walking into this troubled situation and remembers wondering, "What are they asking me to do? Get in the middle of a riot?" But she agreed to come. Students were given Joyce's book *Marked by Fire* to read before she spoke. When Joyce arrived, she was happy to see that the two groups of students were talking with each other about the book. "In this conversation, they found out that they had a lot in common," says Joyce. "They felt the same way about some of the things that happened to the main character, Abby." That day, Joyce feels, she helped two groups of kids who thought they had nothing in common start to build  bridges. She's glad she went, because it reinforced her belief in the importance of literature.

## GROWING-UP YEARS

As a child growing up in Ponca City, Oklahoma, Joyce remembers reading everything. "If it was in a book, I'd read it," she says. "I had no taste at first. After a while, I began to realize that this book was better than that book." Her favorite books were Shakespeare's plays and the Bible. "Some of my friends said, 'that old fogey stuff!'" she remembers. "But I always valued it. I knew it had power."

Joyce also gained a deep love of folktales from listening to the "porch-sitters" in her hometown—older people who whiled away evenings sitting on their front porches, telling and retelling stories of the past, stories about each other, and stories of imaginary creatures—powerful heroes and cruel villains.

Her elders taught her many other things as well, including quite a bit about herbal medicine. She remembers her mother helping cure her fevers and colds as a child by brewing pots of what she calls "broom-wheat tea." "It's good for what ails you," says Joyce. "Especially when it's poured by loving hands." A few years ago she named an anthology of poems *Brown Honey and Broomwheat Tea.* Imagine her surprise when she told her aunt the name of her new book and found out that the proper name is broom *weed*, not broom *wheat*. She laughed at her mistake and then thought about it.

Poems *by* Joyce Carol Thomas ✦ *illustrated by* Floyd Cooper

She had never seen the word written and had only heard it. Joyce reasoned that this is how stories and words changed when passed down in an oral tradition.

## LISTENING TO THE SPIRIT

Many writers say that they get ideas from an inner force they call a muse, which influences them and provides them with energy. Joyce calls her muse "a spirit." "It's so much a part of me that I find myself listening for it and having it guide me to do the right thing, to write a book that I hope will resonate for people," When the spirit is working for her, she adds "I just feel this guidance."

Joyce sometimes takes notes when she is going to write a story. "I keep little cards in my purse and in my car," she says. "Thoughts will come. Often I write down the thoughts and put them in a folder called Ideas. Later, I look back at them."

She doesn't work from an outline . . . at least, not from one that is written down. "The only explanation I can give for this is that I must have a subconscious outline going on in my head," she says. "I tap into it and take my direction from that."

## A WRITING ACTIVITY
### from Joyce Carol Thomas

"I always try to teach my students not to take the accepted way of looking at something but to look deeper. Do not accept what your eyes see or what tradition has told you to believe. If you look deeper, you might come up with an entirely different conclusion than the one you started out with." For example, think about a rock. A rock has not always been a rock. If it is a sedimentary rock, it once might have been a plant or an animal. Try to look at a familiar object in an unfamiliar way. Write about the object from this different point of view.

## WRITE, REWRITE, REWRITE AGAIN

Joyce rewrites each of her books at least ten times. "That's because I keep going back and filling in details," she says. "When I tell students that I write ten drafts, they gasp. I explain that writing is a process." Usually, English teachers approach Joyce after her talks and thank her for emphasizing that point. "Kids think you just sit down and write a book like you write a letter, and then it's over," she says.

Joyce's editors are familiar with her process of filling in more details. She wrote a story called "Young Reverend Thelma Lee Moses" for *A Gathering of*

*Flowers,* a multicultural anthology she assembled. Joyce sent the manuscript of her story to her editor. "Then I got some more details," she remembers, adding that she sent in four drafts in all. "My editor said to the associate editor, 'Put that draft in a drawer. There are more coming. This is the way a *real* writer works.'"

*"I keep little cards in my purse and in my car. Thoughts will come. Often I write down the thoughts and put them in a folder called Ideas. Later, I look back at them."*

Joyce admits that not everyone works the way she does. "Nobody has to work the way I do. You don't have to write what I write. Write what's inside of you."

## FEAR NOT

A very important part of Joyce is her fearlessness—that fearlessness that brought her in front of a group of students who didn't get along with each other. That fearlessness is with her every day. With it, she has driven safely through tornadoes and faced many other dangerous situations. It even guides her at home. "I have a woodpile behind my house," she says. "I'm always out there, picking up wood and bringing it in." One day, one of Joyce's students visited. [She teaches creative writing at the University of Tennessee.] "I sent him out to the woodpile for wood," she says.

The student said, "Don't you know there might be snakes in that woodpile?"

Joyce answered, "If I want fire, I'm going to have to get the wood. If there's a snake in there, I'll talk to him. I want fire. I don't want fear. ∎

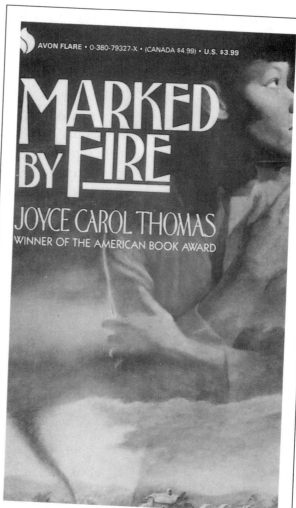

## SPOTLIGHT ON:
### *MARKED BY FIRE*

Abysinnia Jackson is born in a cotton field in Oklahoma. Later in her childhood she is scarred by a spark from a brush fire. She grows up under the influence of Mother Barker, a neighbor and healer who teaches her the mysterious powers of plants and faith.

# Patricia Wrightson

**BORN:** June 19, 1921, in Lismore, New South Wales, Australia
**CURRENT HOME:** Maclean, New South Wales, Australia

**SELECTED TITLES**

**I Own the Racecourse!**
1968

**An Older Kind of Magic**
1972

**The Ice Is Coming**
1977

**The Dark Bright Water**
1979

**Journey Behind the Wind**
1981

**A Little Fear**
1983

**Night Outside**
1985

**The Nargun and the Stars**
1988

**Moon Dark**
1988

**Balyet**
1989

A young Australian girl, newly moved to a remote town in rough hill country, decided to visit her nearest friend one day. The three-mile walk to her friend's house took the young girl across all types of country. At the end of the walk, she had to cross some wide creek flats that had been plowed for corn. "This was the most boring part," she wrote. "I stepped across the brown, loamy furrows thinking of other things—until I happened to see a black snake lying in the bottom of the next furrow."

Black snakes are among the most poisonous animals in Australia, and Patricia was very afraid. She didn't know what to do, at first. "When you meet a snake, you stand quite still and look for a way around it," she wrote. "I stood still and looked. There were black snakes lying at a little distance in the furrows to the right and left. There was a snake in the furrow behind. Now that I saw them, there were snakes in the furrows farther ahead. There were at least six black snakes immediately around me. . . . I couldn't even panic; there was no room. I could only stand."

In that moment, Patricia realized that "the snakes had not attacked me while I blundered in among them; there was no more reason for them to attack me now." She walked slowly and carefully through the cornfield, giving each snake plenty of time to slither away before she got to it. "That was how the country itself taught me to walk as the countryman does, slowly but firmly, giving the snakes time to get out of the way."

Years later, she reflected on this memory and on many other childhood experiences of the wild, untamed Australian bush. She believes that it was her experiences in nature that showed her what her country meant to her. "I don't think any of this made me Australian, but it made me want to be Australian." *(Material in the preceding passages taken from Patricia Wrightson's autobiographical essay in* Something About The Author *autobiography series, published by Gale Publishing Company.)*

## BEGINNING TO WRITE

When Patricia Wrightson first began to write for children in the 1950s there were no Australian children's books. Most books were imported from England. If a few children's books had been written in Australia, they sounded as if they had been written by British writers. To Patricia, filled with her memories of the specialness of Australia, this did not seem right. She wondered if she would find what she was looking for by exploring the myths and legends of the aboriginal people who have lived in Australia for thirty thousand years. By researching these stories, Patricia began to find inspiration to tell her own types of tales, many of which combine the mystery of the ancient Australian landscape with current questions and concerns. By blending the past and the present together skillfully in such masterpieces as *The Nargun and the Stars, The Ice Is Coming, Dark Bright Water,* and *Journey Behind the Wind,* Patricia helped invent modern-day Australian children's literature. Of this she says: "I seem to respond a lot to landscape, so it's pretty certain to have influenced my work. But discovering some of the traditions of aboriginal Australians—traditions that had grown out of the landscape, as traditions do in part—that certainly made the impact much stronger. My sense of country and the work I've done have gone on feeding each other."

*"When I write on paper, it soon becomes illegible; so I've been captured by the wordprocessor, where it's easy to alter constantly as you go along."*

Although legends of the past have served as inspirations to Patricia, elements of everyday life come into the mix, too. She says: "When I make up a character or event for a story, it has to be made up from bits of real life—but not just the way they really happened. It's like making compost out of real life and then growing beans in the compost."

As Patricia writes, the world

A PUFFIN BOOK

The Nargun
and the Stars

PATRICIA WRIGHTSON
WINNER OF THE HANS CHRISTIAN ANDERSEN MEDAL

The Nargun has woken
from its millenial sleep.
And it's coming for Simon.

## SPOTLIGHT ON:
### THE NARGUN AND THE STARS

Perhaps Patricia's most well-known American work, it is still (to the frustration of her fans) not as well-known in this country as it might be. It is the story of Simon Brent, who is sent to live with two distant elderly relatives when his parents die. As the lonely, shy boy gets to know his new home, he discovers mysterious creatures that live all around. The troublemaker Potkoorok lives in the swamp, and fairylike Turongs nest in the trees. Simon soon realizes that his family is aware of the spirits, too. There is also an evil presence: the Nargun, a huge, sinister rock that has been slowly creeping over the Australian countryside since time began, causing mayhem and death wherever it appears. In the end, risking their lives, Simon and his relatives figure out how to drive the Nargun away.

disappears. "What I need for work is privacy and quiet," she says. "I once went on working intensely with a wastepaper basket on fire at my feet and the room full of smoke; my father came rushing in to take control and put things right. I noticed but didn't really notice."

## TOOLS OF THE WRITER

When Patricia is exploring a new idea, she takes notes. "It's the best way to find out if the idea will work, and whether it's an idea for a novel or only a short story." She rewrites constantly. "When I write on paper, it soon becomes illegible; so I've been captured by the wordprocessor, where it's easy to alter constantly as you go along." Still, she's

not convinced it's a good way to work, so when she gets to a difficult part of a story, she goes back to pen and paper.

At some point the writer knows when the story she's working is coming together. For Patricia, that time comes when she finds herself "inside" the piece.

Patricia doesn't know whether or not she's always liked to write, but she does remember first thinking of herself as a writer when she was about eight years old. "Then (quite suddenly, it seems) I was deeply involved in it: writing po'try [sic] all the time, jealously guarding my school essays from interference by anyone else." She started writing a novel when she was eleven, "but it only got as far as one exercise book full when it petered out. I've forgotten what it was about."

*"A novel is only as good as its characters. And the characters are only as good as their dialogue."*

If you hope to be a writer yourself, Patricia advises: "Spend a lot of time listening to people. Listen at school and in the street and in buses and trains. Get used to the different ways that different people speak; hear the rhythms of everyday speaking, and how the beat changes in different moods." Patricia believes firmly that the one most important element in a novel is the characters. "A novel is only as good as its characters," she says, "and the characters are only as good as their dialogue."

On the other hand, Patricia believes that not everyone should be urged to consider themselves as writers. "We need readers as much as we need writers," she says, "and a lot more of them. I am puzzled when it seems that schools and teachers assume that every child can be a potential writer. Why? No one assumes they can all be potential plumbers or doctors or architects; we wait to see, and when it seems justified, we offer support." ■

## A WRITING ACTIVITY
### from Patricia Wrightson

Be alert to lessons you can learn from landscape. Take a walk around an area near your home. Bring along a notebook and a pencil. Stop along the way. Sit down. Write what you notice. List the sounds and the smells. Back in class, record what you experienced in three paragraphs.

# Jane Yolen

**BORN:** February 11, 1939, in New York, New York
**CURRENT HOME:** Hatfield, Massachusetts

The author of more than 110 books, Jane Yolen writes in a messy room. "Books are piled up all over," she says. "Papers, too. My husband once called it my own private nuclear disaster." But Jane knows where everything is, and she takes great delight in cleaning the room after she finishes each book.

Probably, the room gets messy because Jane is involved in so many projects at the same time. Recently, she looked around her workroom and offered this description of its contents: "There are a whole lot of books on the desert. That's because I'm writing a desert picture book, which will be a companion to *Welcome to the Greenhouse*. It's going to be a poem.

"I also have books on covered bridges because I'm doing a covered bridge book. I have books on John James Audubon because I'm writing a book on him from the point of view of one of his sons. It's about a time in his life when rats ate all of his drawings. He lost ninety bird paintings!"

How does this prolific author keep track of her ideas? "I keep an idea file," she says. "I always scribble down ideas when I get them. I find that so many ideas come to me that if I don't write them down, they're gone."

## INSIDE MERGES WITH OUTSIDE

When Jane is writing a book, she is often inspired by something outside herself, which sometimes merges with

## SELECTED TITLES

**The Gift of Sarah Barker**
1981

**Heart's Blood**
1986

**Devil's Arithmetic**
1988

**Best Witches**
1989

**Dragon's Boy**
1990

**Children of the Wolf**
1993

**Welcome to the Greenhouse**
1993

**Sacred Places**
1994

**Passager**
1996

notions from her imagination. Recently, she has been writing a book about Merlin, the magician who was King Arthur's teacher. The book is called *Passager*. A passager is a hawk that's been caught wild and trained, for people who want to go falconing. The book is about a time in Merlin's boyhood when he is abandoned, and left to live in the woods. He is then captured and brought back into human society.

## WORDS FROM THE AUTHOR:

*"It's important to keep open your sense of wonder, your sense of curiosity, your sense of exportation. I think good writers have to be in touch with that openness—that willingness to be surprised."*

sticking-them-on-the-shelves stage," she says of the early research phase. "Some are in the one- or two-line stage. Others are one or two pages long, still others are one or two chapters long." She has written four or five chapters of several young adult novels but has put them away because "I'm not sure where they're going."

Though she's always written rapidly,

"He has no language when he's found, or very little language," says Jane. "He calls himself Boy. He has no name, because he had no one to talk to. When the falconer, who becomes his friend, brings him back from the woods and trains him, he mentions that one of his three birds is called a merlin." Suddenly, the character Merlin remembers his name. "It's as if all of his life rushes back. As he recovers his name, he recovers his memory."

Jane's imagination became inspired by this notion of Merlin losing the ability to talk. "As I get older, I tend to forget people's names and remember faces. So when the idea for this book came to me, I realized it had to be written."

## MANY PROJECTS AT ONE TIME

At any given time, Jane has ten or fifteen books in progress, in many stages. "Some are in the picking-books-up-and-

A PUFFIN BOOK

JANE YOLEN

Children of the Wolf

Can two girls raised by wolves ever learn to live as human beings?

## SPOTLIGHT ON:
### THE GIFT OF SARAH BARKER

Sarah and Abel long to spend time with each other, but are forbidden to talk to each other. Both are Shakers and, in this religious sect, contact between men and women is taboo.

Jane surprised herself by writing *Passager* in only three weeks. "I just sat down and I couldn't get up. Normally, a book like this takes months and months," she says.

## WHAT'S IMPORTANT?

Perhaps the biggest influence on Jane's writing is the oral tradition of storytellers. The sound of words is important to her. "I read everything out loud. So I think, instead of seeing pictures, I am hearing the story as music."

Jane admires many other writers, such as Patricia McLachlan ("every line of hers is a poem"), Diana Wynne Jones ("who can tell the most magical tales"), Bruce Coville ("for his inventiveness"), and Natalie Babbitt ("for the perfection of her work"). But the three authors she says influenced her most worked in the past: Rudyard Kipling, James Thurber, and Isak Dinesen. "All incredible storytellers," she says.

The setting of her books is important to Jane, even if she sometimes chooses a location that makes her uncomfortable. Her novel *Children of the Wolf* is set in a lush jungle in India. "It's fascinating, but terribly alien to me," she says. "I'm terrified of snakes. I prefer a starker atmosphere, like the Scottish Highlands. There's a starkness, a spareness, a cleanness of line that I find more appealing to live in. I need a colder, clearer, cleaner, more breathable line between myself and my landscape."

## THE EARLY YEARS

Jane had what she calls "a very safe childhood." This interests her because "I tend to write in my novels about unsafe childhoods." As examples, she cites her books *Dragon's Boy*, set in King Arthur's day, and *Devil's Arithmetic*, set in Poland in the 1940s.

Happy endings are also important to Jane. "When somebody invests a lot of time reading a novel, if it is terribly bleak at the end, it's like hitting the kid over the head with a two-by-four."

As a child, Jane remembers sitting on

a window seat overlooking Central Park in New York City, reading, reading, reading. Her favorites were *Little Women, The Wind in the Willows*, and *The Jungle Book*. But the books that influenced her most as a child were the Flower Fairy series by Andrew Lang. "I collected all of them and read them over and over," she says.

> *"I really consider myself a storyteller. . . . For me, story is the overriding factor. But I hope that underneath my stories there are themes or visions that my readers will carry on in their lives."*

Jane was, in her own opinion, "a consummate city child." Born in New York City, she lived there until the age of thirteen. She loved going around town on her own. Many of her childhood years were spent at the School of American Ballet, an outstanding ballet school in New York City and a training ground for many future dancers in the New York City Ballet. Jane was a very enthusiastic dancer, with tremendous energy. But as she grew to her full height, her body was inappropriate for a career as a ballet dancer. She was not tall enough, nor slender enough. "I went from being the best dancer in the class to not being good enough, in just six months," she says.

Though she was disappointed with this turn of events, Jane wisely turned to other things. At first, she thought she might become a choreographer. Then her family moved from New York City to a small town in Connecticut. "It was the end of that part of my life," she says. "I have two sections of growing up."

Leaving New York City was a blow to Jane, but she soon adjusted. Music became a bigger part of her life. She got along well with everybody at her new school because "I had a really fast, cynical mouth, and everybody thought that was funny," she says.

Writing was always part of her life, too. In high school and college, she often wrote her papers in verse. Eventually, she began writing books, suffering crushing rejections at first. Finally, her first book was accepted. She hasn't stopped writing since.

## ABOVE ALL, A STORYTELLER

Jane hopes that her readers will come away from her books with a strong sense of story. "I really consider myself a storyteller. I do professional storytelling. For me, story is the overriding factor. But I hope that underneath my stories there are themes or visions that my readers will carry on in their lives." ∎

# A WRITING ACTIVITY
## from Jane Yolen

Take an old folktale, one you know really well, and retell it from a different point of view. Reread "The Three Billy Goats Gruff," for example, and tell it from the point of view of the troll, or of the bridge over which they are trotting.

# Paul Zindel

**BORN:** May 15, 1936, in Staten Island, New York
**CURRENT HOME:** New York, New York

**SELECTED TITLES**

**The Pigman**
1968

**My Darling, My Hamburger**
1969

**The Pigman's Legacy**
1980

**To Take a Dare**
1982

**A Star for the Latecomer**
1985

**The Girl Who Wanted a Boy**
1985

**The Amazing and Death-Defying Diary of Eugene Dingman**
1987

**A Begonia for Miss Applebaum**
1989

**The Pigman and Me**
1992

**Loch**
1994

Paul Zindel once said: "The best writing has to come from being alone with yourself, particularly at the beginning and particularly at the end." He was asked recently what he meant by that statement. "At the beginning, you have to have a vision," he says. "And the closer that vision is to a dream state, the more exciting and vital it is to you." This is one of the reasons Paul writes in the morning. "I'm less intruded on by the world. It seems like a time when I can think the most clearly and feel closest to the dream state."

Privacy is important to Paul later on in the process, too. "It's important at that section in a story after I've done some structuring, some research, some writing, and some studying up on a problem. Then I have to go back into myself to be on the alert for the insight, the epiphany of the piece I'm doing—the answer to the problem I'm writing about." If he has enough private time just to think, he usually gets the breakthrough he's looking for. "Eureka! It comes in." But Paul can only make this type of breakthrough when he's got enough privacy. "It can't happen at a rock concert or while I'm talking to a whole bunch of people, when I'm fragmented and so bombarded by stimulus from the outside that I can't hear the voice inside." When he finally hears that voice, he can think clearly and complete his work.

## ALWAYS A STORYTELLER

Paul remembers that as a boy growing up on Staten Island, he invented lots of stories. "I spent hours by myself. I made puppets. I loved to make little stages and light them with batteries and move things around." Sometimes he would put on ghost shows for the other kids in the neighborhood. "I liked to scare them," he says. Though he enjoyed the recognition he got for the shows, he was a shy person. He says he would have done those shows more often "if I were more brave."

Paul thinks that if a parent today saw a child playing the way he did, they would recognize a possible storyteller. "But if they had noticed me at the time, they would have said 'he'll never make a living at that!'"

When Paul was a junior in high school, he collaborated on an essay for the school newspaper. "That's how I learned that if your writing is printed, you can receive as much applause as if you were a baseball hero." This was a pleasant surprise to him.

In spite of these early successes, he didn't plan to be a writer. "Everbody told me to be a chemistry major so I could become a chemist," he says. Ironically, when he got his chemistry degree, there were no jobs in that field! He taught high school chemistry for a number of years and "eventually my storytelling won out." He says the meandering path his early career took "gives you a good idea of how non-directed I was. I stumbled along and finally, I was lucky. I found out what I was supposed to be doing all along."

BY THE AUTHOR OF *The Pigman*

PAUL ZINDEL

The Pigman & Me

ESCAPE! PAUL & JENNIFER!

### WORDS FROM THE AUTHOR:

*"Writers write compulsively because they really are solving problems. They have this instinct to divide a problem up into little people within a story and move them about into physical events until an answer is served up."*

## GUIDED BY MENTORS

Throughout his life, Paul has had heroes he looks up to who have taught him and helped him out at key moments. "My first heroes were Captain Marvel, Superman, and Batman," he says. "My next hero I didn't know was a hero. It was a man we called Nonno Frankie, who was the spirit that influenced the Pigman character." At the time, Paul didn't realize how important Nonno Frankie was to him. "He was a simple man who worked at the National Biscuit Corporation. He really gave me a lot of qualities that helped me survive growing up without a father," says Paul.

Paul's next heroes were teachers. "They gave me a stability I didn't have at home. I really looked up to them. I admired them."

> *"[Teachers] gave me a stability I didn't have at home. I really looked up to them. I admire them."*

In the next phase of Paul's life, he started meeting what he calls "the celebrity people." This began when he took a writing workshop with playwright Edward Albee and several others. "In a sense they helped me in ways that were unheroic," says Paul. "When I got to know them, I found out they were just plain people, though some of them were tremendous characters." Knowing them helped Paul realize that he could someday be as successful as they were.

Having been inspired by so many mentors, does Paul realize how much of an influence he's had on other writers? He does, though he's quick to add his belief that the whole group of young adult writers have influenced each other. "I was asked to write for this age group at a time when nobody was describing what kids were doing," he says. "I think I spoke with a kind of realism that was a complete change from the kind of books that were being written at the time."

He's glad that so many other writers have entered the young adult field, which arguably, he invented (though he

## A WRITING ACTIVITY
### from Paul Zindel

Once I was visiting my sister. She pulled out an old pile of family photographs. I looked through the photos and found a whole missing two years of my life. I went through and picked out photos of my past and growing-up years that were of interest to me. I took those and photocopied them and made a montage of them. Hidden in that montage was the story that eventually evolved into *The Pigman and Me.* This is something you can do, too. Go through photo albums and pick out pictures from your past. Photocopy them, make a montage, and look in there for a story. Write a story based on pictures from your past that appeal to you.

would credit J. D. Salinger, as well). "There's room for everybody," he says. "As writers, we want to create our own worlds. We get frightened of other writers, sometimes. We're afraid their world is going to be deemed better than ours. But after we've all been around for a while we can realize: 'Gee. All our worlds made it.' We've got enough worlds on our shelves. So now we can enjoy each others' work tremendously."

## FINDING STORIES IN THE FIELD

These days, Paul travels to research his books much more often than he did previously. Recently he was at Stonehenge in England doing research. "I walked around with my tape recorder. I went to ruins of castles. Everywhere I went, I asked people, 'Did anything unusual ever happen here?'" He went to a sixteenth-century inn called the Haunch of Venison and asked his question. They said, "Yes, we were doing renovations four years ago, and we found a severed hand in the wall." Paul said, "That's incredible!" and they said "It's right there, at the bar." Paul went to check and he found a mummified severed hand, under glass. "I could never invent that," he says. "I couldn't dream up the Haunch of Venison Inn either, not in a million years. And it has such a ring of authenticity to it!"

For the book, Paul is trying to create a monster character, which is difficult for him to do. "I'm having trouble manifesting a monster in myself," he says. "I have to find a demon in myself that fits Stonehenge. I don't know what the face of it is, yet, but my ears go up every time I hear about any sort of

## SPOTLIGHT ON:
### THE PIGMAN

In this sad yet humorous story, teenagers John and Lorraine take turns narrating the story of their friendship and their relationship with a sweet, lonely old man named Mr. Pignati. John and Lorraine are welcomed into the old man's home. Without stopping to think about the consequences, the youngsters end up taking advantage of him. By the conclusion of the story, John and Lorraine have learned a lesson—the hard way—about life and death.

ungodly creature." He's excited about the book he's working on, because it is taking him in a new direction. "I'm moving into adventure stories now," he says. "I'm almost becoming old-fashioned!" ■

# Acknowledgments

Thanks to all the authors, and to librarians at Southworth Library; South Dartmouth Massachusetts; Alice Stern, Young Adult Librarian at the Boston Public Library; and the staff at Simmons College Graduate School of Library Science, Boston, MA.

PHOTO CREDITS

Avi: David Guillete, courtesy of Avon Books; James Lincoln Collier and Christopher Collier: courtesy of Bantam Doubleday Dell; Robert Cormier: Jill Krementz, courtesy of Bantam Doubleday Dell; Chris Crutcher: courtesy of Bantam Doubleday Dell; Paul Fleischman: Becky Mojica; Will Hobbs: Jean Hobbs; M.E. Kerr (Marijane Meaker): Zoe Kamitses; Julius Lester: courtesy of Penguin; Janet Taylor Lisle: courtesy of Orchard Books; Margaret Mahy: Beverly Studios, N. Z.; Gloria D. Miklowitz: courtesy of Bantam Doubleday Dell; Nicholasa Mohr: Phil Cantor; Michael Morpurgo: Ron Sutherland; Katherine Paterson: Jill Paton Walsh; Richard Peck: Don Lewis; Robert Newton Peck: courtesy of Bantam Doubleday Dell; Todd Strasser: courtesy of DeLacorte Press; Paul Zindel: courtesy of Bantam Doubleday Dell.

# Notes

# Notes

# Notes

DEBORAH KOVACS is the author of many books for children, including *A Day Underwater* (Scholastic), *Brewter's Courage* (Simon & Schuster), and *Moonlight on the River* (Viking). She lives in Massachusetts with her husband and two children.